Finding Faith Today
How does it happen?

Finding Faith Today
How does it happen?

John Finney

British and Foreign Bible Society
Stonehill Green, Westlea, Swindon SN5 7DG, England

First published 1992

Unless otherwise stated, quotations from the Bible are from the Good News Bible, published by the Bible Societies/HarperCollins © American Bible Society, New York, 1966, 1971 and 4th edition 1976.

A catalogue record for this book is available from the British Library
ISBN 0-564-08475-1

Printed in Great Britain by Biddles Ltd., Guildford, Surrey.

Cover design by Adept Design, Aylsham, Norwich

Bible Societies exist to provide resources for Bible distribution and use. The British and Foreign Bible Society (BFBS) is a member of the United Bible Societies, an international partnership working in over 180 countries. Their common aim is to reach all people with the Bible, or some part of it, in a language they can understand and at a price they can afford. Parts of the Bible have now been translated into over 1,900 languages. Bible Societies aim to help every church at every point where it uses the Bible. You are invited to share in this work by your prayers and gifts. Bible Society in your country will be very happy to provide details of its activity.

CONTENTS

PREFACE

"Evangelization needs to be founded upon fact rather than fantasy." These words taken from John Finney's personal epilogue reveal both the motivation for and the value of this project.

It takes a sample of those in England over 16 years of age who have recently made a public profession of faith, and studies the lessons to be learnt by the Church today from their experience.

It will be immensely valuable for all who are concerned to evangelize during the last decade of this millennium. There have been many critics of the Churches for announcing a Decade of Evangelism or Evangelization. Some have scorned it because they see no evidence that the Churches have an agreed understanding or strategy of evangelism. Part of the purpose of the Decade was to acknowledge this, and to discover by prayer and study how we could be more faithful witnesses to Jesus Christ together.

Churches Together in England are grateful to John Finney, to the members of his Monitoring Group, to Bible Society and in particular to Pam Hanley, its researcher, for producing such a valuable report. It should help us to be self–critical, encourage us as we see how in fact adults are brought to a public profession of faith today, and therefore help us to plan for the future.

We are also grateful to the students of the Anglican, Baptist, Methodist, Reformed, and Roman Catholic theological colleges/seminaries who carried out interviews.

It is an ecumenical survey and much can be learnt from our different ways of evangelizing. Those surveyed include Christians who have professed their faith in a very wide range of Churches. It is providential that the Decade coincides with the renewal of our work for Christian Unity; for unity is not an end in itself, but "so that the world may believe". Evangelization is hindered by conflict and lack of co–operation between Christian Churches. Unity is served by joining together in evangelization.

Those who wish to profit by this survey will have to read carefully the Appendix, or at least the Introduction. To understand a survey of this kind it is important to understand its basis. All research has its boundaries and this survey is limited to those aged 16 and over. It shows the need of the Church to research more fully in other areas, for example the evangelization and nurture of children and the factors which turn people away from the Church. There is scope for much more research in this field and I hope that a group may be established to encourage and monitor it.

However nothing can take away the value of this particular research and I warmly commend it to all who are seriously concerned about the evangelization of England today.

The Revd Canon Martin Reardon
General secretary, Churches Together in England
June 1992

INTRODUCTION

Christians have two unique stories to tell. The first is the story of Jesus Christ. The second is the story of how we ourselves experience God.

In 2 Corinthians 3.3 Paul describes new Christians as letters from Christ.

> "You yourselves are the letter we have, written on our hearts for everyone to know and read. It is clear that Christ himself wrote this letter and sent it by us. It is written, not with ink but with the Spirit of the living God, and not on stone tablets but on human hearts."

Each new Christian is a love letter from God. Love letters are to be treasured, read, and reread. The Church often rejoices in the human being who is the letter without reading it and seeing what can be learnt.

For the first time on a national basis a survey has gathered together the stories of many individuals to see what they can teach the Church. This book is a report of that survey.

The research sought to discover and learn from the spiritual journeys of those who had become Christians and made a public profession of faith in the recent past. They came from every denominational background and many had virtually no link with any church previously.

More than 500 people took part. For most it was the first time that they had had an opportunity to talk in an ordered way about their faith. They found it helpful to trace the hand of God in their lives. Indeed we hope that this survey will encourage church leaders to look at the new people in their congregations and see what lessons can be learnt from them — possibly using the sort of questions used in the survey. Locality was a significant factor in the research. We found that the responses in rural areas varied from those in the town, those in the inner city from those in the suburb. The statistics in this book are mostly average figures from many parts of England, though significant sociological and regional differences are pointed out.

The intention of the survey was more than casual interest in a fascinating subject. We are now well into the Decade of Evangelism (Evangelization). It is important to see what actually happens when somebody makes a profession of faith. What happens in their lives beforehand? What is the effect of encountering the Christian church? What difference does it make to their lives?

This survey will form a sound basis on which churches can build a strategy for sensitive evangelization. Too often churches have relied upon the latest idea or tried to impose a formula which is too tight a straitjacket for the variety of human experience. Much time and money has been wasted because the facts on which this essential strategic thinking could be based were not available.

The history and the methodology of the survey are described in more detail in the Appendix (see page 112), but some points need to be made now:

Criteria for participation in the survey

- We asked a random sample of churches to give us names of those aged 16 or over who had "made a public profession of faith in the last twelve months" (i.e. between about March 1990 and March 1991). We defined this "public profession of faith" as baptism, confirmation, or reception into membership of a church community. It was important to have these objective criteria or the subjective assessment of church leaders might have determined the people we interviewed.
- For Roman Catholics who were baptized or confirmed as adults there were no problems. However, since Roman Catholics are generally baptized and confirmed as children we needed an additional definition of "public profession of faith". We decided to ask for people who had completed a Rite of Christian initiation of Adults (RCIA) course.

RCIA

For Roman Catholics the usual way to initiate new members is the Rite of Christian Initiation of Adults, a process lasting between six months and two years. It is a process of evangelization and catechesis. The candidates first enquire into faith, then explore Christian belief, then grow in a spiritual relationship with God. Finally, after being baptized or received, they are supported as they find a place in the parish and live their faith to the full. Each stage of the journey is marked with public liturgical celebrations. The RCIA is a community process involving the candidates, their sponsors, friends, and families.

- On the other hand the Baptist and New Churches (often called House Churches) baptize all who confess Christ as Saviour and Lord whether or not they have been baptized as infants. Therefore they have more "public professions of faith" (according to our criteria) than churches which do not allow this. (Some would query the term "re-baptism" and it is not used in this book.) Corrections have been made to allow for these anomalies but they need to be borne in mind.
- The survey interviewed those who were aged 16 or over when they

made their "public profession of faith". Therefore it does not cover those who look to childhood as the foundation of their Christian life. This was deliberate. An increasing number of people are being "surprised by joy" as they encounter Christ as adults. An example of this can be seen in the Anglican Church: a generation ago confirmation was primarily a rite for children, and less than a quarter of those confirmed were adults — now half are people over the age of 16. With the decline in the number of those who encounter the Christian faith through the church in childhood an understanding of how people come to faith as adults is increasingly important.

Ethnic background and gender of participants.

- The ethnic background of participants was about the same as that recorded in previous surveys of churchgoers: 95% were described as white European with 4% Afro–Caribbean and 1% Asian.
- The male/female ratio was also about the same as has been recorded in previous surveys of churchgoers at 35:65.

Use of language in the report

- What do you call a vicar, priest, pastor, incumbent? Unimaginatively we settled for "minister" as a catch–all phrase — except when we are quoting what people said. All the way through we have had to use these rather banal words to describe the rich diversity of terminology used by the various parts of the Christian church. To those who encounter unfamiliar words and phrases we can only apologize and say that an ecumenical esperanto has not yet been invented.
- To call the people who were kind enough to take part in the survey "respondents" seemed too cold and "those who took part in the survey" was too lengthy. We decided to call them "participants".

Reading the stories of over 500 participants and seeing the work of the Holy Spirit in their lives has been a privilege. Many of the stories are moving, not because of their melodramatic qualities, though there are some of those, but because of their very ordinariness. We wanted to find the normal as well as the unusual. Often a testimony printed or spoken is of a spectacular turning to God, but most of us come to God by a less exciting path. The straightforward narratives of typical churchgoers are the stories from which we can learn most.

A national project which spans three years and involves several hundred people is indebted to many. The organizations which funded it are set out in the Appendix (see page 112): without their help the project would have been still–born. The British Council of Churches (later

Churches Together in England) gave steady support throughout and enabled the project to get off the ground. Bible Society gave of their money, their staff time, and their expertise in an exemplary way. Pam Hanley as our researcher gave her skills and her commitment to the project as did the people who helped with the interviewing.

The names of those on the Monitoring Group which had oversight of the project are given in the Appendix. They were far more than administrators. They prayed and worked to make it all happen and when this report was written they made detailed and most helpful comments on successive drafts. The mistakes I have made, however, are not their fault.

Above all, our thanks are due to the churches which agreed to take part in the survey and the people who were prepared to unfold their stories in order that we might learn. We are deeply grateful to them and to the Holy Spirit whose work in their lives we sought to chronicle. They are the stars of the show. Wherever possible we have let their own words speak for them.

There are no recommendations in this report for these can concentrate attention on those matters which the author finds interesting. In your own situation there may well be other points in the report at least as striking, significant or strategic. As you read I pray that you may discover whatever is important for your own understanding of the ways of God and humankind and for the evolving mission strategy of your church.

This survey will have done its work only when opinions previously held by all traditions in the Church are challenged by the facts and, where necessary altered in the light of them. Our prayer is that the churches evangelize more effectively and intelligently in ways which are more attuned to the work of the Holy Spirit.

CHAPTER 1

Who did we ask?

We gathered names and addresses of people who had made a recent profession of faith by:

1. Writing to the ministers of 601 Christian churches selected at random from the national denominational lists for England asking for a list of people who had made a "public profession of faith" in the last twelve months.
2. Contacting a further 416 churches — this time choosing more from the Roman Catholic, Afro–Caribbean, and New Churches (House Churches), which had made a lower response to the first enquiry.
3. Writing to 80 more Roman Catholics, since it was particularly important to obtain a statistically valid number of Catholics who had completed the Rite of Christian Initiation of Adults (see page 107). This supplementary survey produced 47 responses.

In total we received just over 1,000 names. We contacted most of these people asking them either to take part in a face–to–face interview or to fill in a self–completion questionnaire. Of the 815 postal questionnaires sent out 360 were returned — a 44% response rate which is excellent given the length (22 pages) and complexity of the questionnaire. There were also 151 face–to–face interviews conducted making a total of 511 participants. (Further details of the methodology are contained in the Appendix on page 112).

The proportion of participants from each denomination is shown overleaf.

THE CHURCHES

To discover something about the participants' churches we gave ministers a list of nine phrases (see Fig. 2 overleaf) and asked them to select the ones which they felt were most appropriate to their church.

Since ministers were allowed to choose more than one phrase the results revealed some interesting overlaps:

- A large number of ministers described their churches as both "middle of the road" and "traditional".

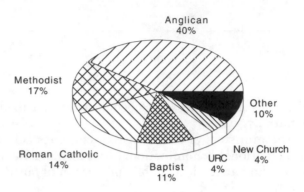

Fig. 1 Profile of participants by denomination.

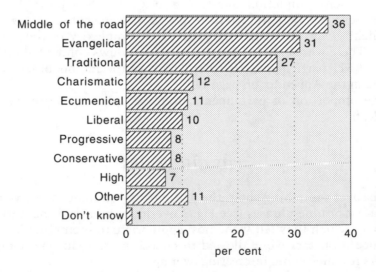

Fig. 2 A description of the churches, as given by the ministers.

- Two thirds of the "charismatic" churches also described themselves as "evangelical" — but a third did not.
- Half the "ecumenical" churches and half the Methodist churches said they were "middle of the road".
- Only about one in ten of the "middle of the road" churches also described themselves as "evangelical".
- Six out of ten "conservative" churches were also "evangelical".
- Anglican churches were less likely than average to describe themselves as either "evangelical" or "traditional".

It is worth noting several other interesting results:
- Methodist and United Reformed churches were less likely to call themselves "evangelical" than average.
- Less than one in twenty Methodist churches said they were either "liberal", "charismatic" or "conservative".
- No Roman Catholic churches described themselves as either "evangelical" or "charismatic" — their usual terms were either "middle of the road" or "traditional". (This may well be because their larger size and general character tends to make them more inclusive.)
- 91% of the Baptist churches said they were "evangelical" and one in four was "charismatic".
- All the New Churches were "charismatic".

There were marked regional differences. Thus:
- 42% of churches in the southeast were "evangelical" (25% in the north and midlands) — with markedly fewer "middle of the road" churches.
- only 5% of churches in the north described themselves as "charismatic" compared with 16% in the southeast.
- 48% of churches in the north said they were "middle of the road".

The social setting
- 55% of churches said they were more urban than rural.
- 18% said they were in an affluent area (29% in the southeast) — more of these were in rural than urban areas.
- 13% said they were in an economically depressed area — most of these were churches in urban areas but 5% of rural churches also chose this description.
- 68% said they were "somewhere in between".

Size of congregations

The smallest congregation was 4 people and the largest was a Roman Catholic church of 2,500.

The overall average was 94 with an average urban church size of 125 compared with 56 for rural churches.

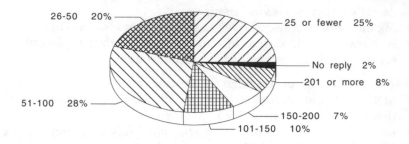

Fig. 3: Size of congregations.

The size of congregation was not so dependant upon social background as is sometimes supposed. Sizes ranged from 87 in economically depressed areas to 111 in affluent areas.

Certain interesting interrelationships emerge:

- only 7% of charismatic churches had congregations of 25 or fewer (compared with 25% of all churches which have congregations of 25 or fewer).
- ecumenical churches tended to have more than 100 people in their congregations.
- evangelical churches tended to have congregations of 51–100 people.
- charismatic, evangelical, ecumenical, and high churches were rather more likely to be in urban areas than rural areas.
- the average Anglican congregation was 81 — 13 less than the average. In part this was explained by the fact that 52% of its churches were in the countryside (44% overall). The Anglicans had fewer churches with a congregation of less than 25 or more than 200 people.
- the average size of Methodist churches was 47. This can be explained partly by the fact that 60% of their churches were in rural areas. 56% of Methodist churches had congregations of 25 or fewer.
- the average New Church attendance was 87.
- Roman Catholic congregations were far larger than the others. 87% reported congregations of more than 100 people and 65% said they were over 200.

In many respects these figures are very similar to those which were published by MARC Europe in the English Church Census carried out in the autumn of 1989. It was reassuring to find that the figures were so similar. We now move into areas which have not been previously researched.

THE PUBLIC PROFESSION OF FAITH

The criterion which was used for determining the sample was a public profession of faith.

This profession could be:
— confirmation or reception into membership of a church
— adult baptism
— the Rite of Christian Initiation of Adults
— some other public declaration.*

*The "other" category included public testimony in denominations which do not have any adult rite of initiation — for example becoming a "senior soldier" in the Salvation Army.

12% of the participants had been through more than one category of profession: e.g. both adult baptism and confirmation or RCIA and adult baptism (see Chapter 11 for more details).

As might have been expected adult baptisms predominated among Baptists and confirmation in Anglican churches.

Apart from three Anglican churches, the Rite of Christian Initiation of Adults was used only by Roman Catholics.

Some important conclusions can be drawn from the statistics:

1. There was considerable difference in the number of public professions in relation to the description the churches gave of themselves.
2. It was important to discover the effectiveness of the outreach of the churches and for this we calculated the percentage of adult professions of faith in each congregation. This revealed some differences between different sizes of congregations: although these were not significant statistically.

The results suggest that a full church tends to inhibit evangelism. This is possibly caused by some sense of complacency or by the fact that the leaders may have difficulty in caring adequately for a large congregation.

The figures are pertinent to the current debate about church planting, whether this is seen as forming new congregations or in having smaller communities within large congregations. They certainly suggest that "smallish is beautiful".

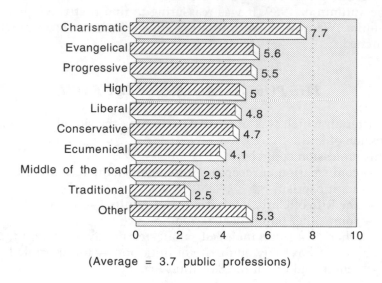

(Average = 3.7 public professions)

Fig. 4 Number of public professions by type of church.

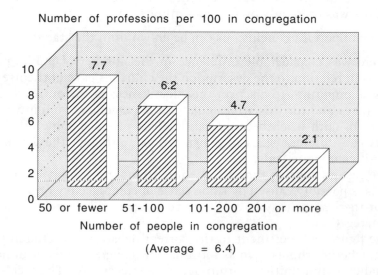

Fig. 5 Number of public professions by size of congregation (church attendance).

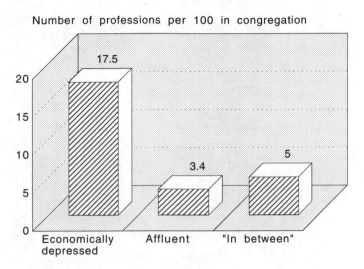

Number of professions per 100 in congregation

Fig. 6 Number of public professions of faith by social setting.

3. The social setting of the churches also produced considerable varia-
tion in the percentage of public professions of faith in any one
church.
The range of descriptions of the social setting of their churches
given by the ministers was very varied so there needs to be some
hesitation in accepting these figures as precisely accurate. But there
is no doubt that they confirm the suspicion which has been voiced
before that churches in poorer areas evangelize more effectively than
those in other settings. Whilst insufficient answers were given to
make these figures precisely accurate, the fact that these churches
often remain small suggests that they have difficulty in keeping
their converts. Either these people drop away from churchgoing
more quickly or they move to suburban churches.

4. Denominationally there are great differences in the percentage of
public professions of faith in a congregation.

5. Since the participants were those who were beginning their
Christian journey they were on average younger than the church
population as a whole.
Younger participants tended to go to charismatic or evangelical
churches. No less than 71% of those in the survey who were under
26 went to such churches compared with 54% of those over 50.

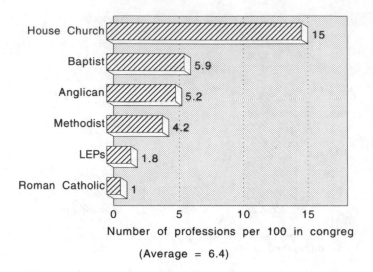

Number of professions per 100 in congreg

(Average = 6.4)

Fig. 7 Number of public professions by denomination.
(The figures for the United Reformed churches were too uncertain to be included.)

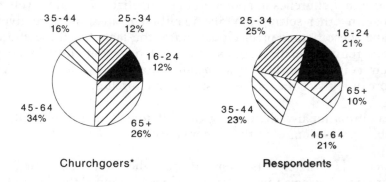

* Attend church at least once a month (Gallup 1991)

Fig. 8 Age profile of participants.

Since the more evangelical and especially the more charismatic churches have more people who profess faith as adults, any survey such as this is going to have a fair proportion of participants coming from those backgrounds. This will become apparent as you read this book and hear the stories of those who have found God.

In many ways, however, this survey does not reinforce what is regarded as a stereotyped "evangelical" experience of sudden conversion. Indeed it puts as many questions to that viewpoint as to every other. There are many in non–evangelical churches who appear to have had such an experience and many in evangelical churches who do not.

CHAPTER 2

Childhood and adolescence

"Boys were more interesting."

"The church started to preach politics instead of the Bible."

"I just drifted away."

"It wasn't the done thing among teenagers."

These are the sort of reasons people gave for stopping going to church when they were young.

We looked at the following six factors in the early lives of the participants and tried to find out what impact each had in later life:

1. Home and family
2. Church and Sunday school
3. Organizations for young people
4. School
5. The Bible
6. The media

(1 to 4 are covered in this chapter, 5 in Chapter 6 and 6 in Chapter 7.)

HOME AND FAMILY

The importance of childhood experiences can be exaggerated and the survey shows that this period in the lives of those who profess faith as adults may not be as significant as might be supposed. The research did not investigate the spiritual journeys of those who made a profession of faith at the age of 15 or under where it can be expected that the influence would be much greater, but only 7% of our participants said their parents or close relatives were the main factor in their becoming a Christian and 23% said it was an important supporting factor. (This is examined in more detail in Chapter 4). Since fewer homes now encourage their children to go to church or Sunday school this fact may bring some comfort: if the survey had found that people were very dependant on their home for their future churchgoing the outlook would be bleak. However the influence of the home is not insignificant.

In the fairly recent past it was usual for children to have contact with a church during their childhood. Sometimes they were brought by their parents who were themselves churchgoers or they were sent by non–churchgoing parents. The number who remained to become adult churchgoers was a small percentage. Young people had contact with the church in their early years and then dropped off in their early teens. But it is clear that the great majority of children now have little contact with *any* church. The recent report by the Anglican Boards of Education and Mission *All God's Children?* found that today only 14% of children have contact with a Christian church during their childhood. If this is an important element in future churchgoing it requires a great deal of attention. The church may need to develop patterns within its life which attract the children, not just of churchgoers, but of non–churchgoers. The church may have done too little in the past to prevent the drifting away of children.

This fall off was generally not due to active parental discouragement. A high proportion of participants in this survey (69%) had been encouraged to go to church or Sunday school and 76% had gone at least two or three times a month.

When asked about their general family background, these future Christians answered:

80% Christian
1% Other faith
19% Nothing

Over half of those described as Christian said their families were Church of England with a further 20% describing their home as Methodist, 10% Presbyterian or Congregational, 8% Baptist and 6% Roman Catholic. As we shall see in Chapter Nine these early denominational allegiances did not always last. There is now a considerable fluidity which means that denominational allegiances are perhaps less strong than they used to be.

Social differences were apparent here. Those who came from a professional or clerical background — ABCIs in the jargon — were more likely to claim a Christian upbringing than those at the other end of the social scale C2DEs. But the difference was not huge — 81% compared with 73%.

However the response "Christian" requires interpretation. It may imply "nothing very much, but not Hindu". The 53% who claimed to come from C of E families may be no more than those who put down "C of E" when they are asked their religion when they go into hospital: it may not represent any great practice of their faith. Although it may not be so marked in the other denominations this nominalism is likely to be true of them also. When they were asked about "your family's general attitude to the Christian faith", the replies were less definite:

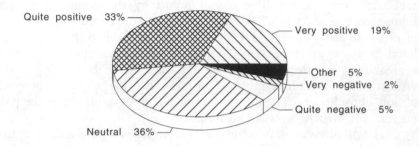

Quite positive   33%

Very positive   19%

Other   5%

Very negative   2%

Quite negative   5%

Neutral   36%

Fig. 9 Family attitude to Christianity.

The survey inevitably picked up those who had been members of Sunday school during the period when large numbers of children were sent by parents who did not themselves attend. The average age of those in the survey was 39 so many would have been children in the 1960s and 1970s or earlier. The younger participants were more likely to claim a positive family background which suggests that they were more likely to have parents who went to church with them. Probably for the same reason these younger people were much less likely to fall away, for it is clear that when children are just sent to Sunday school by non–attending parents it is highly unlikely that they will continue much beyond their early teens: parental example and the other pressures which are upon them pull them away. However if parents go to church their children are much more likely to be able to resist the siren voices of adolescence.

The importance of early encounters with the church can be seen in the figures for those who had no contact with the church. Only 10% never went to Sunday school or church and another 13% went only occasionally. Thus 76% of those who became Christians as adults had a reasonably prolonged contact with a church during childhood — this is a good deal higher than the population at large.

A lot of the families which were described as "Christian" did a reasonable amount to help their children to grow in the faith. This is reflected in the figures about going to church or Sunday school:

69% felt themselves encouraged
15% felt their parents were neutral about it
8% never discussed it
and 2% were discouraged

Boys had not been encouraged to go to church as much as girls. Even at this early age a marked gender difference had begun. This was true throughout the survey — there were about two women participants for every man — reflecting the proportion amongst churchgoers in nearly every denomination. The reason for this disparity is one of the most important areas for future research: the finding in this survey about parental encouragement can only be a very partial answer.

The Church cannot be wholly blamed for the teenage fall off. On the whole the people in the survey had had a reasonably positive experience of church and those who went to Sunday school found it a generally pleasurable experience. Nearly half always or usually looked forward to going and only 11% disliked it, though for some reason which is not immediately apparent younger people were markedly less enthusiastic. The rest varied. It is likely that their attitude towards ordinary school on a weekday was not very different.

But it did not last. 70% of participants who had an experience of the Church as children left, most of them between the ages of 10 and 14. Most had attended for a good spell before that — seven and a half years on average. The reasons for leaving differed. Of the 70% of participants who left church as teenagers:

- 18% spoke of other interests — "looking after two horses", "joining a cycling club etc.". "I thought there were better things to do" was the opinion of a man who left at the age of 12.
- 16% described it as boring. This violent opinion from a woman who had left when she was 12 was not typical:
  "Used to be forced to go . . . hated it . . . it didn't stimulate me at all, it did nothing for me . . . it was the most boring place on earth. Attending adult services was the same."
  It is interesting that this was only felt by a smallish minority: popular mythology tends to regard these early experiences as being dull. It says much for the faithfulness of stalwart Sunday school teachers down the years that this is not generally true.
- 15% moved house and did not continue going to a church in the new area. Younger people mentioned this frequently reflecting the greater mobility of the population in recent years.
- 13% mentioned peer pressure: "It wasn't the sort of thing that

young people did."

- 11% started work or college — "just drifted away, started nursing."

ORGANIZATIONS FOR YOUNG PEOPLE

Many of the participants in the survey had belonged to at least one other organization which was more or less closely allied with the church.

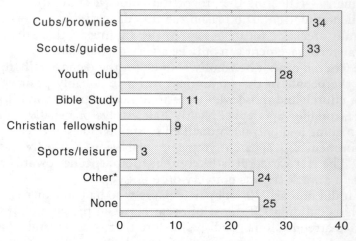

Fig. 10 Church related organizations attended.

These organizations varied greatly in their effect on the Christian understanding of those who went. 39% thought that they had made little or no difference. Most described the spiritual effect of such organizations as scouts and guides in very neutral terms: "I went for the activities — for what I could get out of it. It didn't effect what I thought of Christianity."

Younger people were more likely to describe these organizations in such terms — perhaps reflecting the fact that fewer scout/guide companies now have close links with local churches.

The uniformed organizations were more likely to be described as having little or no effect on Christian understanding than the more specifically Christian groups which met for Bible study and fellowship. A Roman Catholic describes his early encounter with such a group:

"I loved the music and singing — thought that prayer with music was wonderful. I thought, 'If this is what God wants, then I want to give it to him.'"

It was clear that for many the organizations had succeeded in conveying a Christian ethos. Further the organization was often seen as associating the church with fun and a sense of camaraderie — and sometimes it was needed:

"I saw the two sides of Christianity, the fun side and the boring side (in church)."

"Guides had a great effect on me (in retrospect). The principles and practice of being a Christian were clearly shown."

"For the Whit Walks everyone dressed up for the occasion and ate ice creams. Brass bands played and the different churches carried banners."

It was noticeable that the quality and the Christian understanding of the leaders were particularly important. One or two saw an individual guide leader or Boys' Brigade captain as personally responsible for showing them the way to Christ, but there were far more who spoke warmly of the commitment and Christian faith of their leaders.

"I was most impressed by two or three key people who were intelligent, rational, and Christian."

"They all set me a wonderful example."

One participant had encountered *"a 'way out' priest who was a lovely man."*

How far young people in organizations should be expected to attend church as part of belonging to the organization is difficult to assess. There were some who resented it: "that put me off, because I didn't choose to go."

Others appreciated it: "I never had an opportunity to go to church with my family so this was important."

The importance of keeping the Christian aspect of any organization pleasurable is clear from many comments, like these:

". . . made enjoyment part and parcel of my belief."

"On occasion straight Bible study was very tedious and boring. I found this unhelpful in later years (i.e. subconsciously I viewed the Bible as boring)."

Most people clearly appreciated the organizations and the time they spent in them. They are a more important factor in preparing the ground for a later openness to the Christian faith than is generally supposed. It is important that the leaders are seen to be Christian and can make the link with the church.

The evidence from both the influence of organizations and children's early experience of church and Sunday school is that they find it difficult to associate God with their real life if church is linked with what is dreary and boring. The "fun" element is important for it shows that God is about life. Churches could examine their provision for young people to see if this is being provided for in both church services and church organizations. Worship for the family needs this ingredient.

SCHOOLS

27% of participants had been to church primary schools, and 12% to church secondary schools, mainly Anglican and Roman Catholic. Some people had a varied experience: one woman had spent her primary years at Jewish, Anglican and Catholic schools!

Our Roman Catholic participants were more likely than others to have attended a church primary school (37%) — but most of them had been to Anglican schools!

Half of those asked thought that not much stress was put on religion at their primary school, whether it was a church or state school. Only 7% thought it had been given a great deal of emphasis — mainly those who had been to Catholic schools. Older people were more likely to say that their primary school put more emphasis on religion than those who had been to school more recently — though perhaps surprisingly there was little difference between the ages at secondary school level.

But how much effect did it have? The responses to this question are shown opposite on Fig. 11.

The impact of attendance at church schools seems to have been considerable but indirect since hardly any participants saw them as a factor in leading them to profess their faith. Church schools were seen as having encouraged many of those participants who went to them towards the Christian faith though the effect of state schools was by no means negligible. The distinction between state and church schools was particularly marked at secondary level.

Church schools, however, are a mixed blessing. They also seemed to do a better job than state schools at putting people off the Christian faith — some of those at church schools resented having "it rammed down our throats". Clearly at church schools it is not so easy to ignore religion.

How far these figures represent the viewpoint of all who go to church schools is of course difficult to say since those in the survey who were put off at school have overcome any early negative experience and become part of the church as adults. It is a field which requires more research.

We are looking at those who have became adult disciples and it is

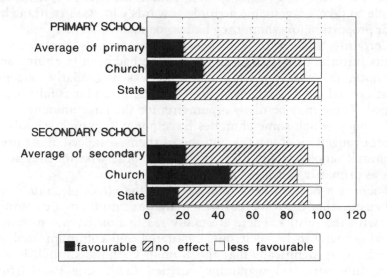

Fig. 11 Influence of school on attitude to Christianity.

probably not right to put too much weight on the remembrance of a childhood which is, for many, far in the past. However it is still remarkable that only one in five on average thought that school made them more sympathetic to Christianity. In the 1950, 1960s, and 1970s when the majority of those surveyed were at school the primary schools would be expected to have a daily act of Christian worship, nativity plays, and for the church schools, considerable contact with the local church.

The overriding impression of this section of the research was that the school, whether it was a church or state school, was only indirectly influential to the Christian pathway of new adult members of the Church. This is remarkable considering how formative these years are and how great a part school plays in them. Not one person thought that their school had provided even a secondary factor in the spiritual journey which led to their profession of faith. There is of course the imprecise but powerful influence of attitudes and values which the participants gained from the ethos of their schools. In most cases memories were not of lessons but of people:

> "The teacher was quietly religious and I still have fond memories of her."

The influence of church schools needs careful evaluation. They may or may not have led many of those under the age of 16 to a living faith and a lifelong commitment to the church. But this survey of those aged 16 and over shows firstly that schools are not a directly evangelizing factor for them, and secondly that church schools in general incline people to take a favourable attitude towards Christianity (though with a fair proportion for whom they had an opposite effect).

Certainly there is no evidence that the schools pressurized their pupils into the Christian faith. Many who had been to church schools did not think that the Christian faith was particularly evident and most saw school as a largely neutral experience as far as faith was concerned. There may be many arguments for the large amounts of effort and money which some churches have put into church schools, but a direct evangelistic impact is not one of them — indeed, most involved in church schools would not wish it to be otherwise for they see their task as primarily educational.

There is a need to keep under review the effect of church schools and ensure that the resources which are put into them are commensurate with the results. There are many reasons for having such schools but they need to be spelt out, evaluated and communicated to the church. (It is significant that the Roman Catholic Church is already doing this with its programme entitled *Evaluating the Distinctive Nature of the Catholic School.*)

CHAPTER 3

Setting out on the journey

What is a Christian?

It is notoriously hard to define the word Christian. Is it someone who goes to church . . . someone who believes in an orthodox faith . . . someone who lives a reasonably respectable life?

The survey had to discover how people defined the word without steering them in a certain direction. They were therefore asked to describe what they understood by it in their own words — possible answers were not suggested.

It was expected that most people would use statements which they considered theologically correct like: "Someone who believes in Father, Son and Holy Spirit" or "Someone who has been born again". A few participants did use this sort of phraseology like the young Anglican shop assistant who saw being Christian as:

". . . believing in God and the events which the Bible refers to . . ."

but they were far fewer than expected and even those who used such terminology often added further comments about what it meant to live as a Christian: for example the shop assistant went on:

"It is very enjoyable and exciting. It means joining in with things and having fellowship. However it can be worrying not knowing . . . what God wants of you."

Only a quarter mentioned that being a Christian was about believing in God and only 4% spoke of the cross of Christ. Nobody said that baptism had made them a Christian and hardly anybody used the word "converted" — extraordinary in view of the denominational spread of those participating in the survey.

This is doubly surprising because nearly all had been through some sort of training course in the very recent past in preparation for their public profession. In most cases this would have contained the use of theological language to describe what faith was all about. It is not that they did not find these courses helpful, for people recorded a remarkably high level of appreciation of them, but few regurgitated the language they had heard — for them the Christian faith is about

19

relationships. This did not mean that they defined a Christian in such vacuous terms as "someone who never hurts anybody". It was much more robust. The central fact was their relationship with God — the rest flowed from this.

Nearly all defined a Christian, not so much by what he or she believed, but in terms of friendship and the effect of faith upon their own life. It is difficult to overemphasize the importance of this, which is repeated all the way through the survey. Faith is seen in terms of a threeway relationship:

  with God
  with other people
  with themselves

Many spoke of their relationship with God:

> "*an ongoing relationship with Jesus . . . peace and security knowing that God is in charge of my life*"

> "*. . . I am not on my own any more . . .*"

> "*living as the Bible tells you, as far as modern life allows you to*"

> "*The Lord with me — and me with the Lord*"

and a young Roman Catholic man spoke of how he had moved away from a formula of belief:

> "*Christianity is no longer a set of ideas set down in books, or rules which must be followed, as in my Jehovah's Witness days. It goes beyond reason, and yet is still real. It means having a personal experience of God. It means having freedom to question, doubt, explore, grow in understanding and faith.*"

A 26 year old woman encapsulated what many participants said about Christian relationships with other people:

> "*loving and helping people, even if you don't want to*"

and many spoke of the significance for them of belonging to a Christian church:

> "*Going to Church means I belong to something and I am not just drifting. I feel I belong to the community.*" (Anglican woman of 23)

In Chapter 9 we shall look in more detail at the difference that people said that being a Christian had made in their own view of themselves. For the moment we need only say that in nearly every case their new-found faith seems to have given them a greater sense of self–worth and they feel more at home in their own skin.

Many speak of achieving a sense of purpose — "before it was a case of drifting". They have found a peace of mind — "I used to be on tranquilizers but I don't need them any more". They feel they have some basis for life — "I know there's more to life than drinking and messing about with girls".

If the experience of the being and presence of God is central to faith then the Church needs to acknowledge it as clearly as possible.

Theological statements which explain the nature of faith appeared to have little impact on the way in which people describe what has happened to them. People look for help in discovering a relationship with God, maintaining it in good repair, and thinking through the difference which it should make in their relationships with others. Perhaps also they need help in evolving a language of their own which describes faith in terms of relationships.

If this is true then the methods used by the Christian Church in its teaching ministry must reflect this. Relationships are not taught in a lecture room. They are learnt by experience, by vulnerability to others, by trial and error. An address about prayer may be far less helpful than the experience of prayer. A sermon about loving your neighbour may be less compelling than an experience of that love.

The Church should do all it can to encourage educational methods which enable people to experience what they learn even if that learning is of considerable intellectual rigour. The Church must present the fullness of God and must do it in such a way that people can enter into a relationship with him, learn about him, and work out the implications of their faith in him.

How the participants saw themselves

96% said that they were definitely a Christian.

The only person who said he was not a Christian admitted to being baptized so that he could get married!

One other person was agnostic: a 17–year–old student said that she now had intellectual doubts — "I am not sure if I believe in God".

We will look next at the participants (just over 3%) who were "not sure" whether they were Christians. This is surprisingly small considering that the word Christian was usually defined in terms of relationships, and we are all aware that these can feel close or distant. Indeed most of this 3% tended to be unsure of their Christian standing because they felt they were not living a very good Christian life. A young Anglican housewife describes this:

"I go to church but I don't feel like a Christian any more. I don't know why but I'm trying to find out."

or another young Anglican who was self–doubting:

"I feel that I do not deserve such a label."

One person had:

"recently restarted attending church because of joining a diocesan Bishop's Certificate course, which has caused a rethink"

and another had been confirmed but:

"I really don't know if I could call myself a true Christian".

One woman felt that there was "something missing", as though she had been through the outward forms of baptism without any inward reality, and she was still searching.

The overall picture of this small group is that a few of them had made a profession of faith and are only now entering into what it means, and that an even smaller number are uncertain of what they have done. Since the survey could come as long as two years after their profession this shows a persistent faith on the part of the other 96%. This was confirmed by the current level of churchgoing — only 1% of those interviewed went less than once a month.

Of those who now called themselves Christians just over half (54%) were conscious of a time when they had not been Christian and of these two thirds described themselves as coming to the Christian faith for the first time: the other third saw themselves as returning to the faith. The number who had been members of another faith was very small — one said she had been a Jew and a handful had been interested in Buddhism or spiritualism though without being formally members of those faiths. The very small number of those from other faiths is an interesting sidelight on the current debate on the relationships between different faiths, c.f. Fig. 12.

There were considerable differences between the denominations in this: 78% of New Church members, 74% of Baptists, and 72% of those from the "ecumenical" churches said that there was a time when they were not Christians — the average was 54%. There were fewer Methodists and United Reformed Church members in this category — 43% and 33% respectively.

Roman Catholics were much more likely to describe their pilgrimage as a return to faith rather than a first time experience (47% as opposed to an overall average of 29%).

Most participants described themselves before this turning to God as "nominal Christians" or used a phrase like "had a vague belief in God" or even "Church of England"!

Of the 46% who described themselves as "always Christian" the great majority had become much more committed in the recent past.

The great range of ways in which people describe themselves indi-

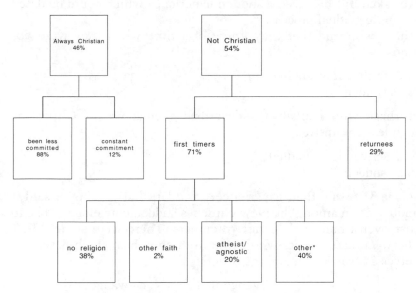

* mainly "nominal Christian"

Fig. 12 How the participants described themselves.

cates that different methods of evangelizing are needed to cover this diversity. We cannot assume that people see themselves as not Christian — even if they do not go to church. This is true even of the New Churches where 22% of those baptized thought of themselves as Christians beforehand.

Many people see themselves as returning to the life of the Church rather than coming to it completely from outside, and this should be part of any invitation to discipleship, not least because the note of returning to the God who they once knew is strongly biblical.

At the same time the need to encounter the growing number of those who have never had any contact with the Christian Church means that it would be shortsighted to go only to the "lapsed". Churches which put most of their emphasis on recovering former churchgoers may need to look more widely.

There were some sociological differences. The lower socio-economic grouping C2DEs were more likely to have known a time when they were not Christians and none of them described themselves as being unchanged by having made a profession. In other words they were more likely to be aware of "before" and "after" than the ABC1s.

The journey to faith — a gradual or sudden experience?

As a preliminary to asking people about the story of their journey to faith we asked if it had been a sudden experience which could be dated or was a more gradual process.

Of those who said that they knew of a time when they were *not* Christians:

X
> 62% described it as gradual
> 38% as sudden

and of those who had always described themselves as Christians (although less committed):

> 80% described it as gradual
> 20% as sudden

X On average 31% said their experience was "dateable", and 69% said it was gradual. Even among the New Chuches sudden conversions rose to only just over a half of their new members. There were some differences between participants who came from churches which described themselves as evangelical and the others:

	Evangelical	Non–evangelical
Gradual	63%	80%
Sudden	37%	20%

The gradual experience was said to take anything from one day to 42 years, though many people saw it as an ongoing process which had not yet finished.

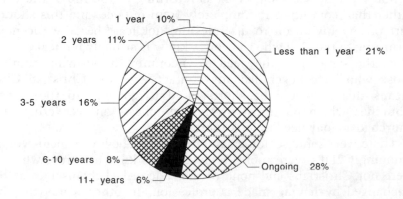

Fig. 13 The length of the gradual journey to faith.

Those who evangelize often look for quick results. This diagram may make them pause. The gradual process is the way in which the majority of people discover God and the average time taken is about four years: models of evangelism which can help people along the pathway are needed.

It is often assumed that younger people are more likely to have a sudden experience and advancing years means that a more gradual unfolding of God is more probable. Surprisingly the reverse is true. The "gradualists" on average began their process at the age of 30 while the average age for sudden conversions was nearly 36. This requires further research.

Most "up front" methods of evangelizing assume that the person will make a sudden decision to follow Christ. They may be asked to indicate this by raising their hand, making their confession, taking a booklet or whatever is the preferred method of the evangelist. The fact is that most people come to God much more gradually. Methods of evangelism which fit in with this pattern are urgently needed. The nurture group and the catechumenate are the best known at present, but others may need to be devised. The use of one-to-one conversations akin to some forms of spiritual direction may be one possibility. Another may be a series of church services where people are introduced to the Christian faith over a period and given an opportunity to respond at each stage. Even more urgently needed are means of helping non–churchgoers to discover God outside the church building in ways which enable a gradual response. *Good News Down the Street* (Wooderson, Grove Press 1982 and *The Church Down Our Street: A guide to everyday evangelism*, Wooderson, Marc Europe 1989) does this but there are few other patterns.

This does not mean that the possibility of "sudden" conversions should be neglected: the figures show that a sizable minority even of those from traditional churches have this kind of experience. Further, the response to a call to commitment may well be a significant step on a lengthy pathway to faith.

Means of evangelism which do not rely so heavily upon the communication of a verbal message are important. Many in the survey clearly received the gospel at a non–cerebral level — through human relationships and pastoral care, through mystery, and emotions. These too are God's ways of evangelizing the world. Is too much of our evangelizing excessively verbose and aimed only at the intellect?

THE JOURNEY — INCIDENTS ON THE WAY

The "gradualists"

To see if there had been any significant staging points in the gradual journey to faith questions were asked about "any particularly important incidents". As could be expected there were a wide range of answers. Some are extraordinary, either because of the distressing circumstances of the people concerned or because of the means which were used to bring relief to them. But most are very ordinary like the Baptist student who confessed that she "wasn't lying on the floor about to die of an overdose but at Spring Harvest". As she remarked, "not very dramatic — but very real".

All the incidents related are moving for they speak of the personal history of real people:

Church events (20%)

The events which were most frequently mentioned were training courses and church weekends.

> *"After approximately one year and a discovery group I heard about forgiveness and understood that if I forgave my ex–wife, the slate could be cleared . . . I prayed with others and felt the Holy Spirit 'move in'."*

> I went on *"a district youth weekend . . . this was the first time I had heard the new songs and realized that God likes drums and guitars as well as organs."*

Meeting Christians (14%)

> *"Chatting over the garden partition I was convinced and what I had 30 years ago in Vancouver when I was converted came back much stronger than ever."*

Going to church (12%)

> *"My daughter asked me to go to church with her and I was pleased to see old friends there from when I used to go — it was like going home."*

> I *"would creep into church but wouldn't let anyone see me — would have ruined my image."*

> *"I went to church on Sunday and was immediately overwhelmed by the love and presence of the Holy Spirit. I cried but did not understand . . . deeper commitment came three months later."*

"I was dragged to church one day — there was a nun who said she went to mass to recharge her batteries and I thought 'Gosh, perhaps there's something in it.'"

"I was at the darkest moment in my life . . . I went to a church parade with the guides that I work with and I was sat in church when I felt something lift the darkness, pain, and guilt, and left me with peace, light, and free from pain, and with so much joy that I felt as if I was dreaming."

"At the singing of 'And can it be' I was drawn to the small wooden cross on the altar table. I could not take my eyes off it and the words of the hymn simply destroyed me. I honestly felt I would die, feeling both incredible joy at being reconciled to God through Christ, and distraught at the price that was paid for me. I immediately asked the pastor to baptize me."

Bereavement (9%)

"My cousin's husband died and his example of faith made me realize that what I had in life was very shallow — so I attended the vicar's study course."

"I had a miscarriage — during the grieving process I realized that something was missing in my life."

"My husband died, my only brother died, my son had cancer. I was distraught. I would not turn to God then as a support — as a prop. I coped with my problems and I felt that I had an inner strength . . . gradually I came to realize that this strength came from the Holy Spirit."

"My sister died — she'd greatly suffered. Made me feel I must go to church and pray."

"My son had a brain tumour and he helped me to see God in a different light even though he was only seven and upon his death I thought only that he was with God in peace."

"I lost my wife and felt I wanted to end my life and asked God to help me . . . he answered my prayers."

Birth of their own children (8%)

Sometimes it was the wonder of new life and the responsibility of it which made people think more carefully:

"Having children changed my outlook on life . . . I became more thoughtful."

Sometimes it was the process of getting the baby "done" (5%)

> *"I wanted to have Diane baptized. I went to one vicar who refused,
> but a second vicar was really nice and encouraged me to start
> coming on special days (like birthdays). Gradually I went more
> often."*

Their marriage partner (6%)

> *"We both felt the need to thank God."*

> *"My husband came back to it first — we had a year arguing about
> it."*

> *"Finding out what love really means so I could understand the love
> Jesus had for me. If my husband could love me that much how
> much more could Jesus love me."*

An evangelistic event (6%)

Answered prayer (6%)

> *"I was in need of some money and I prayed and when I got home
> there was a note and I had to phone a number and when I did I was
> told that I had been given £5,200 . . . the money enabled me to
> make a new start."*

> *"I was on the point of having no home, no money, a 3 year old and
> a baby. One night I was at the end of my tether . . . I had been
> praying and the words came, 'be still and know that I am God', and
> I slept. People helped, money arrived from nowhere and I was put
> on a completely new path."*

> *"I was trapped in a freezer and I knew that if God didn't send
> someone to free me I'd die — I prayed and I was released. It started
> me thinking."*

> *"My daughter had a brain haemorrhage . . . which left her
> paralyzed and epileptic. This was about twelve years ago. She was
> given approximately ten years to live. She fought it with the help of
> medication and has now returned to work . . . As an elder at the
> church she was asked to do a reading at the Christmas Day service.
> While she was reading I had a feeling of being hugged and of
> someone at the side of me. I burst into tears and said a prayer of
> gratitude for such a miracle. I feel this is when it happened for me."*

Their own baptism/confirmation (6%)

Contact with a minister (5%)

". . . coming across an extremely communicative powerful vicar . . ."

An illness (5%)

"I had to cope with debilitating health problems and there was no one to talk to about it . . . so I turned to the Lord."

"Everything caved in and I'm told I spent six weeks in hospital. It was a long, long dark tunnel. I then started to think of the Lord and Jesus and with the help of my wife and church members I saw that there was light and hope . . ."

" . . . a second heart attack when I 'died' physically. When I recovered I opened a book I had partially read. The next chapter was 'How to come back to life and enjoy it more'!"

Reading the Bible (3%)

Others mentioned:

"World crisis started to make me think."

"During the Gulf Crisis my uncle was posted to Saudi Arabia with the USAF and I was worried for him."

"Giving up cocaine, cannabis and various other narcotic and hallucinogenic drugs — and giving up the way to pay for them."

" . . . stopped trying to gain money by insurance work — offering a receipt that was more than estimated. I found I couldn't receive money falsely."

"I was working in Saudi Arabia where the constant attacks on Christianity made me start wondering and searching."

The Jehovah's Witnesses deserve a special mention. The following is typical of several comments:

"I had new neighbours who were Jehovah's Witnesses and I read much of their literature and listened to their beliefs, that I thought

*were beautiful. But then I questioned many things which were
impossible to live up to, some being ridiculous in my thoughts, so I
turned to my Bible to check their comments and beliefs and found
there was no reference to them . . . God answered my prayers and
many things became clear to me."*

Sometimes people give a whole raft of events which led them onwards.
An Anglican househusband of 42 lists those which helped him:

*"A friend sent me literature and letters exploring what Jesus meant
. . . someone pushed a leaflet into my hand while out shopping . . .
a Cliff Richard song made me listen and cry 'Share a dream
with me'
. . . the vicar asked me to attend an evening service."*

A 37–year–old woman mentions:

*" . . . my time at university when my flatmate was Catholic . . .
then being married to a cradle Catholic . . .
thirdly, the birth of my own children . . .
and the death of various members of the older generation."*

She concludes:

*"There was a crystallizing process . . . brought on by these
experiences of birth and death".*

A "crystallizing process" describes exactly what many experience. A
great deal is happening in their lives, some of which is perceived with
hindsight as incidents along the way, but much more is unseen and
unknown. Many describe the process as "searching" or "being confused". It may continue for years until something leads to the "crystal-
lization" — this may be someone asking them to come to church, or a
dream, or an evangelistic event. This "crystalizing event" leads to a
clear sense of things having begun to coalesce and what had been frag-
mented becoming whole. This in turn leads people to ask for baptism
etc.

Our understanding of this "process" and the "event" is crucial to
evangelism. It begins by helping people on their journey. The above
examples show the diversity of means by which this takes place. The
most useful help seems to be given by friends and ministers who are
sensitive to what is happening and reflect it back to the person concerned. Time and again appreciative comments are made about friends
who did not preach but simply reassured them that God was in it all
and gave support and encouragement.

To force the pace is counter–productive (remembering that the average time for a "gradual" journey to faith is four years). There was a marked aversion to the "pushy" person who tried to push forward their own ideas.

The other part of evangelism is offering "crystalizing events" where the process comes together. These may well not be events which are intended to evangelize. The evidence shows that many of them are no more than a sentence or two spoken to the person concerned, or an ordinary church service, or an act of friendship. However, this is where evangelistic events may have their value. They are not seen as a main factor in their spiritual journey by many people but they can provide a focus for what has been happening in their lives for some time.

The "conversionists"

Those who had had a sudden experience of God were asked what happened. Again there was a wide range of answers. The commonest were:

Bereavement (18%)

> *"A friend was dying. He had recently become a Catholic. The peace he found and the care of the church impressed me. He had had a very hard life with no spiritual help until he became involved with the local Catholic Church . . . Three days before he died I felt a deep call to be a Christian while the parish sister was praying with us at his bedside."*

A church service (18%)

> *"I was praying by myself in church: 'Why can't I come in?' and to my great surprise and disbelief I heard God answer 'You are in'."*

During prayer (13%)

> *"I had a nervous breakdown and attempted suicide. I saw four angels who prevented me and gave me something to live for."*

> *"I was sexually abused as a child by my father — at 50 years of age I forgave my father on a special night: I love him now and told him I forgive him now."*

Preaching (12%)

An evangelistic event (11%)

The influence of a minister (8%)

> *"A vicar showed compassion after the death of my wife".*

Reading the Bible (8%)

Talking to Christians (6%)

Divorce (5%)

Their own illness (5%)

The main difference between the experience of those coming gradually and those having what seems a single episode is that the latter tend to be much more overtly religious. Evangelistic events and the Bible are more important. Preaching was hardly mentioned by those on a more gradual journey but is important for those who come suddenly. Conversely the "human" factors — friendship, the birth of children etc. had less effect. There was one noticeable exception to this — bereavement was mentioned by twice as many having "sudden" experiences as those coming to faith by a more gradual process. Perhaps the suddenness of death sparks off sudden reactions.

THE BACKGROUND TO THEIR JOURNEY

It is often said that people only turn to God from a position of weakness so we wanted to find out what was happening to the participants — both the external circumstances of their life and how they were feeling within themselves.

Externals: what was happening to them?

To see if there were any particularly stressful events occurring at the time of their turning to God a question was asked about "anything particularly important happening in your life". The most common events mentioned were:

14% bereavement — particularly mentioned by women
9% breakup of marriage or cohabitation
8% getting engaged/married — particularly mentioned by men
8% having children — particularly mentioned by women
8% moving home — particularly mentioned by men
7% fear for others
6% their own illness

Remembering the length of time that the "turning " can take, this cannot be an unusual collection of events, though the incidence of bereavement and divorce is possibly higher than could be expected. It is interesting that people put down positive experiences like having children or getting married as well as the negative.

Internals: how were they feeling?

People were asked what their state of mind had been at the time while they were turning to God. Of the participants who described themselves the following are the most usual words used:

25% normal
17% depressed and unhappy
14% confused and disturbed
11% content and happy
9% questioning

In all about a third said they were unsure of themselves and in need of help: some described themselves as depressed or even suicidal. In certain cases it was clear that the externals of their life had caused this: e.g. a bereavement or illness, but it is clear that many were going through a period of life when they were looking at themselves and not being satisfied. For some a "confused unhappiness" is probably the best description. But besides these there were many who were searching in an adult way for handholds for their life, and who were accepting the inevitable confusion which is part of this process. Still others had nothing very much happening to them — they were simply going through life without any dramas.

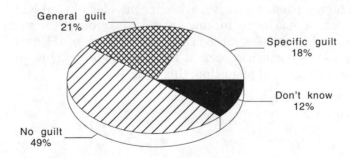

Fig. 14 Awareness of guilt.

Consciousness of sin and guilt

Since much evangelistic practice sees repentance as a precursor of faith and tends to define repentance in part as being sorry for what we have done wrong, questions were also asked about "any sense of guilt or shame".

Only 39% said they had *any* sense of guilt — about half of these were ashamed of one particular thing, while the others had a general sense of shame. Perhaps surprisingly there was virtually no difference between the sexes and the over 50s were less likely to feel guilty than those who were younger. The proportion of those feeling no sense of guilt was somewhat lower among Roman Catholics and those from ecumenical churches and higher among New Church members.

While the forgiveness offered in the gospels is clearly important to many it is not the overriding factor for most. The picture of guilt–ridden, self–accusatory people finding psychological release by turning to Christianity is sometimes painted. If it is true at all, it is true for only a small minority — the great majority of the stories which the participants told did not fit this pattern.

Presentation of the gospel which expect a consciousness of sin or a sense of guilt in the audience do not touch many, and do not speak at all to the majority of those who are present. Thus to present the cross as only a means of forgiveness is to narrow the full breadth of its meaning. For most it is likely that at this early stage in their pilgrimage the cross of Christ finds its main significance in revealing the depth of the reconciling love of God.

Consciousness of God and prayer

The survey tried to discover whether the idea of God had come out of the blue or had been lurking in the background for some time. For quite a few it was clear that the Hound of Heaven of Francis Thompson's poem had been at the gates awhile. "How much had you thought about God just before this time?"

23% a great deal
42% quite a lot
30% not much
5% not at all

This went along with a questions about their practice of prayer. "How frequently did you pray before you became a (more committed) Christian?"

25% every day
15% every week
35% less often

6% only in emergencies
15% never

This agrees roughly with other less detailed surveys that shows that about 60% of the population claim to pray "regularly". Those in this survey seem to pray about the same amount. Prayer is such a common experience, even among those who have no practice of churchgoing that the ways in which we can evangelize by helping people with their prayer life needs to be explored. While prayer is common the person or force to whom the prayer is addressed needs to be explained. Paul in Athens saw the altar inscribed "To the Unknown God", and proceeded to introduce the unknown deity. The church has a similar opportunity now.

CHAPTER 4

Factors leading to faith

One of the most important parts of the research was to find out what people saw as important in their becoming a Christian. We were well aware that the most important factor is the work of God, but what means does the Holy Spirit use?

Those in the survey were first asked what they considered to be the main factor which led them to become a Christian (or a more committed Christian). They were given thirteen possibilities but were invited to write down anything which was not listed. (The thirteen were chosen on the basis of earlier research.)

They were then given the same list of thirteen possibilities and asked if any others were also of importance. They could choose more than one. We called these the "supporting factors".

The results look like this:

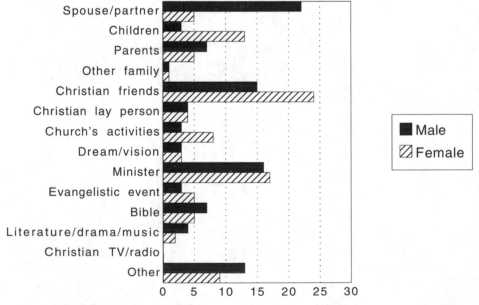

Fig. 15 Main factors in journey of faith.

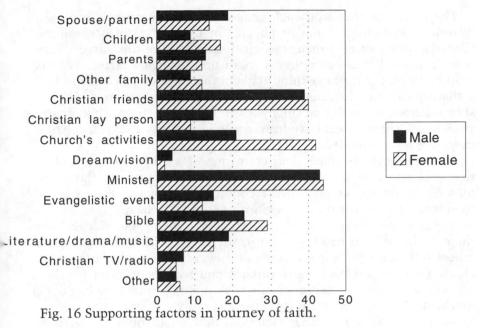

Fig. 16 Supporting factors in journey of faith.

Since participants were able to indicate more than one supporting factor the percentages in Figure 16 do not add up to 100% — direct comparisons with Fig. 15 have to take this into account.

("Other" factors included a vast range of suggestions — "God", "myself" etc. In particular bereavement and contact with other beliefs was mentioned by several participants).

There were no significant differences between socio–economic groups, apart from "church activities" which ABC1s found rather more important than C2DEs.

Similarly there was remarkably little difference between those in rural and urban churches. In the supporting factors there is no statistically significant difference at all. Among the main factors rural churches found that Christian friends and the minister were somewhat more important and the influence of children rather less, but the differences were not great (e.g. the minister was important for 20% in rural churches and 15% in urban churches).

Denominational differences were much more marked. Baptists are four times more likely to find the Bible a factor in their conversion story than average. Roman Catholics are very successful in influencing their partner. 44% of New Church members are brought to God by their friends. Anglicans rate their minister as being particularly significant in their faith journey. The ethos of each denomination is reflected — the Catholic emphasis on the family, the Baptist stress on the Bible, the New Church teaching on lay witness. It needs the whole church to evangelize the whole world.

The recent emphasis on such charismatic phenomena as healings, "words of knowledge", and prophecies in the process of becoming a Christian does not get much statistical support from this survey. Very few mentioned these as either a main or supporting factor. This is despite the fact that a large minority said that they themselves had had a charismatic experience either at the time of their turning to God or soon afterwards, and that many of them came from charismatic churches. Claims which have been made for this style of evangelizing may need to be modified.

As in the findings about their definition of a Christian it was clear that once again the personal is much more significant than those factors which do not involve direct contact with people. For example friends and family are more widely influential than the media.

It was in this section of the research that many individuals told their stories of what had happened to them. Some are straightforward, others tell of much heartsearching and eventual release. All are precious. There is something unvarnished and real about them for they are ordinary people explaining in their own words what God has done for them. Much can be learnt from them.

We look now at the other factors which are mentioned above or under "other":

Family
Christian friends
Church activities
Dreams and visions
Bereavement
Contact with other beliefs

("Minister", "Evangelistic events", "Bible", "Literature/drama/ music", and "TV/radio" are discussed in detail in later chapters.)

THE FAMILY

Partner

(This might be a marriage partner, or a boy/girlfriend — live–in or otherwise.)

22% of men had found that their partner had been the main factor in bringing them to God.
Only 5% of the women said the same.

> "When someone you love and respect starts talking about something you oppose it makes you think about it."

The two things mentioned by this 43–year–old Roman Catholic are crucial. First a basic relationship of "love and respect" and then a readiness to talk about faith. Without the former talking sounds like nagging and without the latter faith seems to be just a private matter. Most Christians who love their partners and whose faith means much to them want to share it like this nurse who had been influenced by her husband:

> "He always believed but then he became more interested. Once we found a road to travel together we went on . . . when we had children we wanted to thank God in some way."

The need to be sensitive and not to impose one's faith is often seen in the replies, like this one from a 44–year–old Baptist:

> "My girlfriend was a Christian, so I thought I'd give it a try although she never forced it on me."

or this from a 61–year–old female shop assistant:

> "I fell in love with a Catholic and under no pressure from anyone changed my religion. This in itself made me a much more committed Christian."

Occasionally, of course, the reverse was true!

> "She left literature around the house concerning Jesus and Christians. Then one day my motorbike wouldn't work, and not being anything wrong with it my wife suggested I pray. And I heard God's voice say 'Put it back together', so I did and it worked. It was so real that on that night . . . I opened the door to Jesus."

Often it was the change in the partner which was most influential

> "I wished to share in the comfort and peace of mind which it obviously brought to my wife."

Nearly one in ten looked to their partner as the main factor in bringing them to Christ but it varied greatly between denominations. It was true of only 3% of Methodists compared with 36% of Catholics. This might be because the Catholic church has paid more attention to the help and support of the family than other groups and emphasized the importance attached to bringing up children in the Catholic faith.

There is a need to give much help to those who are partners of someone who is not a Christian. The witness of one partner to the other appears to be one of the most influential means of evangelism, particularly the witness of women to men.

Few churches give much help to Christians whose partner is not a Christian. In such a personal subject many questions arise and possibly one–to–one counselling needs to be offered. Discussion in groups may invade the necessary privacy of a relationship with engaged or married people discussing their relationships without the presence of their partners. The best group training may be role plays and teaching on human relationships.

Their own children

3% of men and 13% of women said this was a main factor
9% of men and 17% of women said it was a supporting factor
We had not anticipated the number who had been brought to Christ by their babies. There seemed to be three possible scenarios:

1.   The first began before birth:

> "*I didn't want to turn up at the vicarage and expect the vicar to christen my child. It was very hypocritical for me to expect him to do. So I started to go to church. If I hadn't been pregnant I don't know if I would have become a Christian eventually or not.*"

2.   The second happens at the time of birth. They are moved by the gift of a new life like this Roman Catholic mother:

> "*I wanted for them what I hadn't had as a child. I wanted them to have the chance of faith. Having your own children gives you a glimpse of God and his love for his children, even when they are turning away from him.*"

It seems to be the very process of birth which people found important: it was difficult to put into words. "In a way God came and told me I was not on my own."

There seems to be more in these experiences than just a wish to bring a child up properly or accepting a new responsibility as parents — parents seemed to have encountered something of the mystery of creation.

3.   The third scene is some time later. The young couple approach a minister (often an Anglican) and ask for the new baby to be christened. For many this was clearly a very important moment, and their reception was all important. The welcome which seems to be most useful is one which combines friendliness and straightforwardness. This remark, in this case about a United Reformed Church minister, was typical:

> "*I wanted my daughter christened and the minister said, 'we don't christen anyone. You must do something.' This forced me to take things seriously.*"

We will look later at the attitude of the minister and the central importance that this has. For the moment we can only say from this evidence that parents need to be offered a pathway towards faith rather than be expected to leap into it.

Churches which baptize infants have considerable divisions about the value of an "open" baptismal policy which makes few demands on the parents or one which demands a clear affirmation of faith from them. Whatever the theological implications the evidence suggests that in practice parents need to be shown total welcome and also a way in which they can find out more about God in their own time. Many spoke of the three or four baptism preparation groups which they had been expected to attend as very formative — partly because they learnt about the Christian faith and partly because they were able to break down their wariness of the clergy.

Further research needs to be done in this area to discover what is helpful to the parents and which method offers them an introduction and invitation to the Christian faith.

Besides the impact of their babies there were parents who had been influenced profoundly by the challenge of their growing children. For some it was younger children who had shamed their parents into going to church:

> "I sent my own children there because I was friendly with the teacher who ran the Sunday school and my children were friends with her girl. I felt it was not fair to send them and not go myself."

> "My children were asking questions to which I didn't know the answers and also telling me things that I had forgotten and I became involved with a Pram Service." (Anglican 40–year–old housewife)

> "I realized that my daughter probably wouldn't become a Christian without some kind of an example . . . " (Catholic housewife of 44)

> "I wanted the best for them and felt this was the right way to do it. To encourage them I attended Family Service once a month . . . I started staying at church each week and enjoyed it." (Anglican woman of 31)

When the research began we expected to find examples of parents who had been brought to faith by the enthusiasm of their children who had found Christ when they were in their teens or twenties. Apart from a few older people who had been taken to church by their children this did not appear to be the case.

Parents

There was no significant difference between the sexes and on average:
    6% said it was main factor
    13% said it was a supporting factor

As might be expected the younger people were when their spiritual turning took place the more likely they were to look to their parents as a formative influence on their faith: for those under 26 the figures were 13% who considered parents to be a main factor and 28% who saw they were a supporting factor.

Even bearing in mind that this is a survey of those who have become Christians at 16 or over many would have expected these figures to be higher. The fact that only 6% said that coming from a Christian home was the most important reason for them becoming a Christian is surprising. Possibly even more remarkable is that only 12% saw their parents in a supporting role, remembering that a parental example of churchgoing has a positive effect. A number of responses showed that people had grown away from their upbringing and had made up their own minds about their faith.

> *"I think that if my parents had not encouraged me when I was young I don't know if I would have gone to church until many years later (if at all)."* (Young Methodist female legal secretary.)

This fits with the earlier findings about the comparatively limited influence of home, school, and youth organizations: for most they had some significance but it was seldom overwhelming. Few of those we interviewed felt that they had had their course set for life by their childhood experience.

Other family members

1% said it was the main factor
11% said it was a supporting factor
Those most mentioned are grandparents, brothers, and sisters. A 21–year–old was helped by her brother:

> *"He has been a Christian since he was 16 and he wrote to me saying that he was getting married. I realized that he was happy and I was not. He showed what I had and what I could have. So I moved to London to be closer to him."*

While these family members are mentioned as a main factor by only a handful of people they are said to have had an important supporting role — almost as significant as that of parents.

> *"My sister really suffered yet was a devout Christian until the day she died and I was amazed someone could suffer so much and still believe . . . "* (Retired Anglican woman.)

Summing up the influence of the family

It is mentioned as a main factor by 27% and a supporting factor by | about half of the participants.

CHRISTIAN FRIENDS

15% of men and 24% of women said this was the main factor |
39% of men and 40% of women said it was a supporting factor |

Both as the main factor in the journey to faith and in helping along the way friends rated very highly indeed — the figures were not far behind those of the influence of the family. They gave love, care, understanding, and prayers.

We asked participants if they regarded one special person as particularly influential or whether it was a group of people. Only about a quarter looked to one person as the key influence though, of course, there may have been one person who had been particularly helpful, or who had introduced them to the group. To belong to a group of friends who were Christians was important. *For most people the corporate life of the church is a vital element in the process of becoming a Christian and for about a quarter it is the vital factor.* Forms of evangelism which fail to recognize this are doomed.

We also asked a question about church activities and while only 6% saw this as a main factor, a third (34%) saw them in a supporting role. Obviously there is much overlap between being influenced by the life of the church and by Christian friends so these figures could almost be added together. We can say with confidence that:

- Christian friends and the corporate life of the church are the main factors for over a quarter of all people coming to faith.
- Nearly three quarters find friends and the church play an important supportive role in the process.

The influence of different ecclesiologies in evangelism can be seen by comparing the figures for New Church members and Roman Catholics. 44% of those entering the New Churches said that friends were the main factor. These churches grow mainly through word of mouth and give much attention to helping the members of their congregations to witness to others: clearly it works. The growth of these churches shows that their emphasis on "every–member ministry" pays off in terms of bringing people to baptism.

On the other hand only 9% of Catholics said that friends were influential. Catholics look particularly to the family and the corporate life of the church to help people to discover faith, and, as we have seen, this is very helpful in evangelizing adults. However the danger of relying on this is that it only evangelizes those who have a Catholic background. In a national situation where many have little or no faith this may not be sufficient.

The life and morale of the church is particularly important because if morale is low among church members they will not ask their neighbour to come to church ("come and get bored along with me", is not very inviting). Possibly many churches need to address this fundamental question along with their mission to their community.

Friends seem to be effective when they are examples of two things — faith and normality.

Faith was seen as a "something extra" which Christians had. It appears like a refrain throughout the responses, though it was clearly difficult to put into words. A debt collector of 27 spoke for many:

> *"They seemed so different. When I was in their presence I felt different than when I was with other people. I realized that I did not have what they had. They had a different outlook and happiness in whatever they were doing."*

Other enthusiastic comments were:

> *"I realized they had something fantastic in their lives."*

> *"My friend seemed so 'at one' with herself she seemed to radiate, even through times of trouble."*

This emphasizes the *difference* that people found in Christians. But faith only seems to be evangelistically effective when it is allied with *similarity* in other aspects of life.

> *"They talked about Christianity as reality, not just a myth. People who are normal people."*

> *"They were my own age and I could relate to them easily, so I could ask any queries and they would find out the answers." (18–year–old Methodist, farm worker.)*

> *"My girlfriend had been a Christian for some time and had tried sharing her faith with me but I knew best and told her in as many words to shut up or leave. Anyway I met some of her Christian friends and I was amazed to find they were normal people, not religious freaks, and I found myself getting to know them and like them . . . "*

A retired Anglican was surprised that the people he had met in the village church were the same as those he met in the village pub:

"My conclusion was that, rightly or wrongly, Christians were in fact human . . . up to then that was not 'allowed' in my understanding of Christianity, but this really was the beginning of my 'new' look at the church and Christianity. Strange, but it worked for me!"

Those making the journey of faith need people with whom they can identify. Very few of those we asked made a solitary journey — there were nearly always others around them. The rest of this section picks out elements of friendship which made it possible for this identification to take place.

An important part of friendship is accepting people despite their own valuation of themselves:

"They supported me without judging and they liked me. I didn't think people did like me before this point." (A woman of 34.)

But a 40–year–old nurse tutor found that not all Christians were equally friendly:

"The vicar's wife befriended me at a time when I needed it and accepted my incorrigible behaviour. (She said, 'You're on our prayer list.' Me: 'How long will it take to work?') She didn't give up. But other friends have also put me off! I had a friend at work who was utterly horrible but went to church."

It was important for friends just to be there when the time was right:

"When I started becoming curious I wanted to talk to someone I knew about it — had close friends who were Christians and I went to them. The second person I asked gave a leaflet to me, invited me to meetings and so on. I went to her baptism and gave my life to the Lord." (16–year–old student.)

"I went to talk to a friend up the road who I had known for a long while. I knew she was a Christian but I had not had much contact with her having left work. I would never have thought of going to church. I asked her what church she went to: knowing what type of person Anne was I thought it would be OK. She asked me to go with her — I was pleasantly surprised." (28–year–old Anglican children's nurse.)

A 34–year–old Baptist found his way back to church:

"I know a group was praying for me. I had taken a holiday from church, but still wanted to know what was going on. Wife still went. I quizzed her and we had a dingdong."

They had also to be the sort of people who were seen to be worthy of trust. A 29–year–old Catholic entertainments manager:

> "*An older person who I very much respect as an intelligent, knowledgeable, and rational man has a very strong Christian faith. I was spurred to find out more about it by the fact that such a man could be so sure about it.*"

Often the link with church was important — the simple "come along with me" was all that was required. One lady of 46 remarked that "this was the first time anyone had actually asked me to go to church" — and had gone the next Sunday. There were a few stories of friends who had "led someone to Christ" — but far more stories of people who had invited their friends to come to church. They had found it helpful and in the fullness of time this had led to them professing their faith. This is a typical story from a 41–year–old Anglican who is now an invalid because of his previous work:

> "*I was listening to the chap down a mine when I was working down the pit. He was telling people that he was going to a meeting about 'waiting on the Spirit'. I asked him what that meant and he explained that a lot of them were being baptized in tongues — the gift of tongues. I asked him to explain . . . I asked him if it would be possible for me to go along to witness what was happening as I was a bit intrigued . . . I turned up at this particular church and we sat in a circle of people. I felt really embarrassed . . . I was praying in silence and I asked if Jesus was actually there would he come into my life . . . I felt a great power from the bottom of my stomach — like butterflies — and it was a really happy feeling rushing up inside me . . . the next minute I was the first one to stand up uncontrollably speaking in tongues. I had never heard anyone speaking in tongues before.*"

Many evangelistic training schemes tend to ignore the church. Training is given on answering fairly stock queries and then bringing the person to a sudden act of commitment. It is difficult to talk about a "normal" pattern when discussing human behaviour but a very common approach to God by someone feeling their way seems to be:

- Seeing an individual or a group of people with something attractively different
- hearing why they are different
- asking questions and receiving answers
- responding to an invitation to come to church or a meeting

These steps ultimately lead the person concerned to become a full member of the church.

Appropriate help needs to be given to lay Christians to give them confidence to take their part in this process.

It is important for Christians not to force their opinions on others. Repeatedly those in the survey say how grateful they are that their own views were respected and that there was no manipulation:

> *"They didn't continually force their opinions and ideas down my throat — which would have irritated me. They showed me their love by befriending me and this was very important."* (Methodist osteopath of 29.)

> *" . . . it is important in those early 'searching' stages that the pastor (or whoever) is approachable and believable i.e. not 'over the top' and not too pushy. This type of person creates the right atmosphere of comfort and relaxation."* (Evangelical sales rep. of 50.)

At the same time prayer is not thought to be manipulative! It is recorded with gratitude — the osteopath concludes:

> *" . . . after I became a Christian I found that many had been praying for me."*

A 22–year–old New Church member found his Christian friends had helped him through a tragedy:

> *"My best friend was killed in a road accident so I went to church on the Sunday to pay my respect. I went every Sunday after that. People were helpful at church, they kept ringing me up and asking me for a drink."*

Many people think that being interested in "religion" is going to make them appear odd, and they are afraid of being laughed at. A 22–year–old student said his Christian friends gave him "safe" surroundings in which to explore:

> *"They provided an environment of a nature which makes you feel as though you are not enquiring into something particularly strange. By strange I mean something that's going to make you look a fool. You can check things out with them which other people might regard as strange."*

If "friendship evangelism" is one of the most natural and effective means of evangelism, are too many churches so over–busy with their own internal life that their members do not even have time enough to look after their own families let alone love their neighbours? Friendship needs time. Every Christian needs to examine the right relation between time given to the life of the church and that given to family and friends.

CHURCH ACTIVITIES

While things that happen in and around church are only seen as the most important factor by 6% they were seen as a supporting factor by 34%. As mentioned before there is bound to be a considerable overlap between this category and that of Christian friends, and even the minister, and evangelistic events, but there are many who look to what happened in a church service or meeting as particularly significant for them.

> *"I sat at the back of church and a member of the congregation found the pages in my ASB (Prayer Book). I whispered that I was not confirmed and could not receive communion. He insisted that I went to be blessed by the priest . . . the emotion I felt on being blessed was overwhelming . . ."* (47–year–old teacher who describes herself as Anglican/Baptist/Methodist.)

This experience of the effect of being "blessed" at a Eucharist is mentioned by several participants.

> *"I thought I'd go along to a meeting (not really believing). During and after the meeting I began to think 'there's something in this'."* (Anglican male surveyor of 28.)

There are many references to the church being "home" and people speak of the sense of security and homecoming when they eventually find their way into a congregation — (this has of course to be balanced with the strangeness of the church culture for those who have never experienced it).

> *"I wanted to join the church community for the support and for the discipline. Being a Catholic is living a whole way of life and that appealed to me."* (25–year–old woman, office administrator.)

Another Catholic gave a similar testimony:

> *"I am concerned at the way society is going and I admired the church for taking a stand against divorce and abortion in particular . . . when I went to my local church it was full and I liked the atmosphere."*

Sometimes there is a sense of a rather lonely wandering which leads eventually to a haven, like this moving story of an elderly Methodist man:

> *"At a fairly early age I began to develop a strong sense of an inner spiritual life. After many years in the Pentecostal church I drifted gradually away from it, finding the rather noisy emotional form of worship a distraction . . . for many years church attendance was very intermittent, though I still believed strongly in the moral*

*teachings of our Lord . . . I have developed a longing for the
fellowship and encouragement of people who still attempt to live
for the things Jesus taught us to covet. This led me to abandon my
'spiritual island'."*

Clearly churchgoing does some people good. A number of people testi-
fy to the marked effect that worship had on those they knew:

*"I noticed that there was something different about my wife when
she returned home from the morning service. I can best describe
this as a warm glow or radiance . . . One Sunday I decided to see
what was going on . . . "* (Anglican aged 59)

DREAMS AND VISIONS

Questions were asked about these because research done by the
Alistair Hardy Institute had indicated that a high proportion of people
had had something "strange" happen to them — David Hay in
Exploring Inner Space (Mowbray, 1987) says it can be as high as 62% of
the total population.

It was only important for a comparatively small number of people —
3% saw it as a main factor and 3% as a supporting factor with no significant difference between the sexes.

A 34–year–old Anglican who worked in an hospital had taken an
overdose:

*"I lay in hospital with everyone running around me and I felt this
real calmness and saw a vision. A 'being' came to me and said, 'I'm
not ready for you yet — I'll call you when it's time.'"*

A 38–year–old unemployed Anglican said:

*"I was on the common and the wind was gently blowing. I was all
alone with just the cattle and the horses. Suddenly I felt a warm
feeling come over me. I distinctly heard my name. I looked round.
No one was there. Again I heard my name. Before I knew what
happened I was down on my knees praying. I felt that everything
was going to be OK. When people saw me they said that my face
was shining. I felt strong and alive. I know that that day God had
spoken to me. From that day on, I have followed Christ."*

*"I had a series of very vivid dreams . . . Jesus took me down a set of
very grand stairs, opened a very large door and guided me to a road
which forked. One fork of the road was not signposted and the
other fork was signposted and said 'Jesus'."* (Anglican engineer of
25.)

Another question asking about this kind of episode experienced by participants found that about a third described something of this sort and these are explored in Chapter 10. It is interesting that those events which occurred before their profession of faith were not seen by most as factors which influenced their actions: they were remarkable and strengthening but they did not compel action.

However a very great number of others mentioned some sort of feeling which had a touch of the divine about it. There are many stories of this kind — often they are associated with a church building or a service.

> *"When I went to midnight mass about two years ago I felt an uncanny peace come over me whilst in the church. I can't really describe how I felt."* (Anglican teacher.)

BEREAVEMENT AND SUFFERING

Many looked back to a time of suffering as a time of change. As we have seen above they frequently look primarily to their friends or the church who supported them, but this is not always the case. Sometimes God meets them directly:

> *"About two years ago I had a miscarriage . . . I felt empty and inconsolable. No family, doctors or friends could help me. I turned to God for help in desperation and from this time I gradually recovered. I felt it was nothing short of a miracle. I went from being desolate to feeling human again."* (Anglican teacher of 33.)

CONTACT WITH OTHER BELIEFS

Contact with Jehovah's Witnesses:

> *"A JW called on me several times at a time when life was beginning to have little meaning for me and I was deeply unhappy. Through her I began to wonder if that was where I had gone so wrong in deserting God. That particular faith did not appeal to me so I decided to go to a Methodist church service . . . "*

A very small number of people had had contact with spiritualism in one form or another. For most it was a thoroughly negative experience. A few had been in contact with occult practices. At times they needed a ministry of deliverance before they were able to be free:

> *"I had been involved with the occult for a long time. I went to a healing centre because I wanted to be free of Satan . . . one day I was set free. I screamed out the name of Jesus and the chains were broken . . . My life since I have been a Christian has changed completely."* (Unemployed Anglican woman of 38.)

CHAPTER 5

The minister

In the last chapter the witness of Christian lay people was seen as being of paramount importance, but the research also showed that ministers are significant not only in the running and the morale of the church but also in the personal lives of the people they encounter, both inside and outside the life of the church.

We were interviewing those who had recently made a commitment to God and the church, and they had often been guided along their personal pathway by a minister. Not surprisingly therefore clergy get a good press. The interest lies in what they are respected for.

Many participants spoke of their feelings about ministers. Those who have not encountered many tend to think that they are difficult to approach, expect them to be judgemental, and out of touch with real life. Possibly this idea comes from the media which tend to portray ministers as either "silly asses" or "tortured souls". Stories also get handed down in families from generation to generation about "difficult" ministers who had a disagreement with a family member many years ago. This retired Anglican had a stereotype in mind when he came across a better example who helped him to Christ:

"He was not the archetypal vicar one usually encounters (beaming, well fed and housed, totally out of touch with ordinary, universal problems)."

There is a similar note of surprise in many of the responses. They expected to meet someone very different. Hence they pepper their answers with words like "friendly" or "approachable" (this was particularly so for women). Although no direct question was asked, no less than 41% of those who volunteered an opinion mentioned that the minister they had encountered was friendly and approachable, and 27% thought he or she was helpful and encouraging.

"He was so down to earth, very normal . . . he took a real interest in me and listened to me too." (40–year–old female Anglican, poet.)

"His honesty, cheerfulness, and general character were important to

me. The way he looked on Christianity as a celebration of life; he had an enjoyment of living." (32–year–old Anglican, housewife.)

"I was stunned by the man. He seemed to be sensible and warm and friendly and his communicating in his preaching was clear . . . this vicar died and I felt I'd let him down by not going further — in a Christian sense. It's as though he had shown me the way but I hadn't followed. Then we moved house to where we are now. This man applied the Bible to life in general and that was important to me." (36–year–old female Anglican, psychologist.)

"She has such a kind sincere face and friendly manner." (Methodist woman of 55.)

"He was outgoing and met everyone on their own terms." (44–year–old computer programmer in an ecumenical church.)

It is noticeable that many of the examples are Anglican. The Church of England has an enormous burden and opportunity. Rightly or wrongly in many areas the vicar is seen as the "official in charge of religious affairs". People turn to him or her for baptisms, weddings and funerals unless they have a link with another church. Many come with virtually no church background, never having talked to a minister before and more than half expect a rebuff. If they find someone who is friendly, glad to see them, and helpful they are both relieved and impressed.

The Church of England is in some part fulfilling this: the number of those who said the minister was the main factor in their becoming a Christian was higher among Anglicans than other denominations. It was also noticeable that there were some whose first contact with any church had been with an Anglican minister and who had subsequently found their home in another denomination.

All denominations, but particularly the Church of England, have great opportunities for evangelism through the "occasional offices" (mainly infant baptism, weddings, funerals). These opportunities for evangelism should be given first priority in most areas. The research showed that many found God through a sympathetic and helpful personal approach — not so much what happened at the service but in the preparation beforehand and the follow–up afterwards. The responses suggest that the order of importance is infant baptism, funerals, weddings.

The number of this type of service in urban areas can be overwhelming and many ministers are uncomfortable about the amount of support they can realistically give. It may be necessary to devise ways in which lay people can also make full use of these opportunities to serve members of the community.

There is no doubt that what is seen as a refusal to help is deeply resented:

> *"The new minister was not keen to baptize someone he didn't know, so I phoned the assistant minister here in tears . . . "*
> (Housewife at an ecumenical church.)

However, a friendly response by the minister can blunt the negative effect of the refusal:

> *"I went to the vicarage to ask for daughter to be christened. He said he would only bless the baby but offered to help with getting to know what the Christian faith is all about."* (33–year–old female Baptist.)

It is likely that there will be no progress in helping someone to faith unless a basic human relationship has been established. Friendship leads to trust, and trust leads to a readiness to accept what the other has to say. Every salesperson knows this truth, and so they are taught how to appear friendly. Nearly all in the survey found genuine friendship from their ministers. Hardly any ministers are mentioned disparagingly.

But the participants were looking for more than affability. The need for personal integrity is spoken of repeatedly:

> *"He was one of those rare people who lived what he preached. A joy came out of him — people sometimes shine. He was a joyful, funny person even when he was serious. He was very gentle, very kind: it just came naturally with him."* (Baptist woman of 35.)

> *"He makes you look at yourself. He's so committed himself; he gets you to realize there's more to be gained from the church."* (United Reformed Church housewife of 42.)

> *"He lived a good example."* (Unemployed United Reformed Church man of 50.)

> *"She had a light shining from her."*

> *"He seemed to be such a lovely person — so joyful even when his life was going through difficulties. One always felt better for having met and talked with him. I wanted to know what gave him that inner sparkle and, if possible, get some of that sparkle for myself."* (Anglican woman librarian of 41.)

Similarities of background were seen as important in making relationships:

Similarity of age was helpful:

"With him being younger . . . .doesn't drone on like the older ones."

"She was a woman of my age."

"Expected to meet an old geyser — young, friendly person answered phone."

"The most interesting thing to me was the two ministers resident here, both of whom were younger than me. I'd never met young ministers with new ideas on old themes." (Retired Anglican woman.)

"Younger than any minister I had met before — or maybe I'm getting older and they seem nearer to my age now."

Similarity of experience and vulnerability was also mentioned:

"We both gave one another support for he too was suffering from stress and depression."

A non–Christian background was felt to be an asset:

"He was not born and bred in the church and can relate to 'lay' life very well."

"He's been through the mill a bit himself. He became a Christian in the RAF in Bahrain. You can relate to someone who has led a bit of a wild life before becoming a Christian. Sometimes I wonder when these 'schoolboy' Christians preach and tell you that life should be rosy. They've never known what it is to have a hard time so how can they know what it's like for those who have." (Male Methodist, 55, unemployed.)

For some the contact with the minister had been because of a crisis:

"I telephoned the local vicar because I had decided to kill myself — I had the day planned. I got the phone number from the telephone directory: it popped out of the book . . . He visited my home two or three times in a couple of days." (40–year–old typist who now is partly Baptist and partly Roman Catholic.)

"I was very ill with no money and the church sent me away to a retreat house to convalesce." (31–year–old man in an ecumenical church.)

One minister "professionalized" the help he gave to a person in trouble by allowing a certain amount of time to them on a regular basis — this was appreciated:

> "He said he would counsel me once a month for as long as it took. He gave me the freedom to be myself. He said I could ring him whenever I liked because he knew I wouldn't abuse that."
> (54–year–old Baptist clerk.)

The importance of being given time was mentioned by a number of participants:

> "The vicar didn't push me — he didn't say I had to come every Sunday — he said, take your time, which I found helpful."

> "He took time out to listen and understood how I felt." (Baptist man of 34.)

> "He was supportive without being pushy." (Roman Catholic housewife of 39.)

> "The pastor visited me several times in hospital in spite of it being quite a long journey . . . it helped me through a very traumatic and worrying time." (Retired Baptist woman.)

For some it was a casual conversation with a minister:

> "I have been for as long as I can remember a quiet, shy person. I never had the guts to attend church yet I always wanted to. One day I plucked up the courage. It just so happened that the priest was sitting at the back of church. We spoke for about fifteen minutes, during which time I told him about my feelings . . . I felt that I had a friend." (Male Anglican policeman of 24.)

> "Whilst walking my dog in the early morning I met another dog–walker who later turned out to be the vicar . . . I started to attend his church . . . and with his help I was able to overcome my diffidence and see my way to faith." (Retired Anglican man.)

For some it was the result of bereavement:

> "When my grandma died it was like a massive chunk gone. Where had she gone? What is she doing? A friend down the road said 'Come to St Matthew's.' I went and felt really light. Went and talked with the vicar . . . I had a lot of questions that needed answering and the Bible helped. It was all positive." (Anglican student.)

"He didn't make me feel guilty that I had come back to church because I had been bereaved." (Anglican woman of 40.)

" . . .because of the death of a very close person the local pastor called without being asked, to offer what help he could. I found this very helpful . . ." (Retired Baptist man.)

"The curate used to come round to the house on the night and just let me talk and we would pray together." (Anglican nurse of 30.)

The importance of bereavement as an opportunity for pastoral care has, of course, always been recognized by the church. However, used with sensitivity, it is also an opportunity to invite people to come closer to God, for they are often asking themselves searching questions about their own lives at such times.

It is noticeable from the survey that this questioning occurs not only among the close relatives (whom the minister is most likely to encounter) but among the friends and more distant relatives who are only in the background on the day of the funeral. The church may need to strengthen its ministry in this area still further.

The teaching ministry of the minister is not unimportant, though it is clearly second to the establishing of friendship. 14% thought the minister was a good teacher and explained things well, and 13% thought his or her preaching was good. Just as women tended to respond to the friendliness of the minister so males looked for good preaching — though the difference between the sexes is not great and should not be overemphasized.

"Monsignor X showed me much more of the Bible's meaning and how God reveals himself to us than I would ever have known without his help."

"More modern sermon, using everyday examples." (Anglican 30–year–old housewife.)

"He is very caring and explains Christ to us in his sermons better than any other preacher I have met." (Retired woman.)

Some spoke of the personal relevance of what was being said:

"It seemed as though she was speaking directly to me when she was speaking during the services. I realize now that it is God talking to me . . ." (Methodist male factory worker of 35.)

"It was almost as if he knew what I was thinking of doing and he was telling me not to. I realized later that God was using him to

talk to me and help me sort myself out." (Male Baptist caretaker of 40.)

One Anglican woman teacher took a strongly cerebral approach (though this was not a frequently expressed attitude):

"He said and still says exactly what I have always felt should be said from the pulpit, although the message is both comforting and challenging. The emphasis is very much on Christianity being a serious intellectual exercise and not frivolous with a great emphasis placed on witnessing."

The minister as evangelist

17% said a minister was the main factor for them becoming a Christian and no less than 43% said he or she was an important supporting factor (there was no real difference between the sexes).

"He made me WANT to know Jesus Christ personally." (Baptist shopkeeper of 51.)

"He had the Lord and I needed him." (Evangelical 59–year–old postman.)

One of the surprises of the survey is the importance of the *personal* ministry of the clergy in evangelizing. It is often thought that the minister's role is to support and encourage lay people in their witness. This may be so but the direct impact of the minister cannot be avoided, and should not be minimized.

The most important evangelistic work of the minister appears to be not in the church and the pulpit but in two other kinds of relationship:

• one–to–one meetings with non–Christians and the "lapsed".
• group situations, particularly those where there is an opportunity to talk about the nature of faith.

In these situations many ministers were incarnational in their evangelism: "he was nice person and he put God over as a nice person", as one Methodist woman said. For better or worse ministers are seen as "representatives of God". They are of course seen as a role model of what it is to be a Christian. More awesomely they are also seen as a reflection of the character of God. If they are stern God is seen as forbidding; if they are open and friendly God is seen as welcoming. As a Catholic man said of two priests:

"They both showed me the human face of God."

The most effective evangelism grows out of an existing pastoral relationship. But friendliness is not enough — it is the necessary beginning of the relationship but it has to be taken further. There is a place for challenge at the right time.

A Church of God minister told a retired man that it was no good sitting on the fence: "at that time I wasn't a heathen and I wasn't a Christian". Or an Anglican minister who "brought home to me what being a Christian really meant", or the experience of an Anglican woman personnel manager of 48:

> *"The vicar asked me probing questions which really made me think about what it means to be a Christian. At times he made me feel uncomfortable, but he also gave me straight answers to my questions and I think this has strengthened my faith."*

Many Christians have known the "holy hunches" which Archbishop Michael Ramsey described — the impulses of the Holy Spirit which push us in a certain way. A retired Anglican woman describes the impact when a minister decided to follow this guidance:

> *"One time, when I was ill, and didn't know which way to turn, there was a knock at the door . . . A vicar stood there and said 'Child, you are ill. God has been telling me all morning to come to you, so I have.'"*

Sometimes the minister is unaware of the significance of what he has said:

> *"It was a chance remark from a visit to the vicar which seemed to make things slot into place."* (Anglican 48–year–old male construction manager.)

Ministers need to be confirmed in the importance of their personal ministry and may need further training in the skills involved in this form of spiritual direction. Ministerial dialogue with those coming to faith is clearly so important that much in–service training is needed.

The other way in which ministers encountered people was in group situations (other than in church). The importance of introductory courses (nurture groups, Rite of Christian Initiation of Adults) is mentioned by a number of participants:

> *"The minister runs a three week course for those who wish to investigate Christianity from an adult's sense and I went to that and I've gone on. The assistant minister also runs a course which they call Christian Basics and that takes 12 weeks and studies different aspects each week — Who is God? Holy Communion, the Holy Spirit etc . . ."* (33–year–old woman in an ecumenical church.)

"When my daughter was becoming the age for confirmation I made enquiries about adult confirmation classes. I attended these classes and I found them very interesting and I thought to myself 'I don't think I really understood the meaning of this when I was younger'. But I certainly do now." (Anglican female assembly line worker.)

Such courses appear to give an opportunity to learn about the Christian faith in a relaxed atmosphere. They also begin to provide the vital personal links with other church members and with the church leadership: learning and fellowship are essential to growth.

Ministers may need help in both the content and the methods of leading introductory groups. Many "enquirers" find these catechumenate type courses a way into the Christian faith and this should be a priority in the training of ministers.

CHAPTER 6

The Bible

Questions about the effect of the Bible during childhood and adolescence produced a very diverse set of responses. There were two camps — a large minority who found the Bible alive and wonderful, and those who found it the very opposite. There were few neutrals — only 20% had no view on the subject.

We asked participants for their views at the time of their secondary schooling which was for most of them long before any "turning to God". For a considerable proportion the Bible was, even at this early stage, an important element in the formation of their Christian understanding, though it has to be remembered that presumably there will be others who are turned away from the faith because of their antipathy to the Bible.

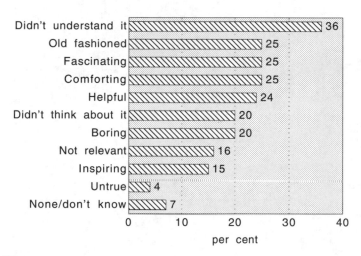

Fig 17

Fig. 17 Phrases used to describe the Bible in childhood and teens.

It is interesting that only 4% thought of the Bible as untrue. Later in the survey when we asked if there were any parts of the Christian message which they did not believe before they became Christians a whole range of uncertainty surfaced from Adam and Eve through to Revelation. Do youngsters accept what they are taught unquestioningly and do "doubts" only surface later in life?

When we went on to look at the part the Bible had played in the period leading up to their "turning to God" 3% of those who had a "gradual" turning found the Bible highly significant:

"I was having Bible study and I liked what I heard."

"I had been through a dreadful time — my marriage had broken up and I was feeling hopelessly lost . . . intellectually I felt trapped — as though I knew that the only answer lay in a spiritual direction which I was unable to know or follow . . . one night I found myself praying . . . a few days later I was suddenly aware that I should read Matthew 13.8 'But some seed fell on good soil and brought forth fruit . . . '. I had not read my Bible for over twenty years, and I believe that was a personal miracle . . . I could begin again."

A higher proportion (8%) of those who had had a "sudden" experience of faith looked to the Bible as significant.

When we asked participants whether the Bible had been a significant factor at the time when they began their faith journey there was little difference between the sexes.

On average:

5% said it was the main factor
27% said it was a supporting factor

Not surprisingly many saw the Bible as a book which was a companion on the way rather than the main factor. However there was considerable difference between denominations. No less than 22% of Baptists said the Bible was the main factor for them. Once again we see the factor which is stressed by their denomination being particularly influential in the lives of their members.

Despite the difficulties which it raised for some it was an important aid.

- It was a well–read book. 47% said that they read it "several times a week" with only 19% saying they read it "seldom or never" during this period of change.
- The great majority (87%) of those who read it thought it was helpful and half of these rated it "very helpful".

A Presbyterian accountant found faith through the Bible:

"It was one authoritative voice of God, and if he wanted to say

*anything this would be how he would say it. Whilst I wasn't
always sure this was God speaking, it always felt like a holy book,
not to be taken lightly."*

It is in this area that intellectual searching is seen as important and
relationships are subsidiary. Elsewhere the reverse is usually true —
the answering of questions is significant but the most important element is a relationship with someone else, though even here some, like
this Roman Catholic piano teacher, mentioned Christian friends alongside the Bible:

*"I saw a pattern in the Bible. I read the Old Testament more than
the New and saw the prophetic side of Jesus, how the old and the
new fitted together. It all clicked, that Jesus was the Lamb of God
— the prophets foretold an event beyond their own circumstances.
Theologically that had more influence. Practically, friends —
particularly one — had more influence in befriending me in a way
no one had before, different to a non–Christian friend."*

Of course the Bible does not only speak at a cognitive level — it also
challenges our behaviour:

*"I was getting drunk on a regular basis. I read in the Bible that you
could choose to serve God or alcohol. I chose God."* (Young Baptist
man.)

And the power of the story of the Bible is still effective:

*"I was reading the Gospel according to Mark. When I read about
the crucifixion I had an indescribable feeling which included a
combination of fear, ecstasy, and awe. I knew that Jesus Christ was
with me."* (Baptist shopkeeper of 51.)

*" . . .I dug out my old school Bible. The words within the gospels
leapt out of the page at me. Two days later I had a 'Road to
Damascus experience' whilst I was driving through the countryside.
Momentarily the bright sun shone through my windscreen and
within that flash of light I accepted Jesus as Saviour."* (Baptist
manager of 31.)

There is a need for straightforward material which can steer those
coming to faith through the Bible so that it is a real support to them at
this time of turning to God. It should be readily available outside
church circles.

While questions raised by the Bible are frequently mentioned, there
appears to be a need for material which deals with very elementary
questions in the whole field of Christian belief and life. When people
were asked about the areas which they found difficult before they

became Christians such subjects as Adam and Eve were mentioned at least as often as more profound subjects. While few people in the survey appeared to be primarily convinced of the truth of the Christian faith by intellectual reasoning, they appeared to have a good deal of "brushwood" which needed straightforward explanations. Some require intellectually heavyweight material but there is also a widespread demand for the kind of interim apologetics which clears away the hindrances to faith for those asking simple questions at a not very profound level.

CHAPTER 7

The media

In an age which is supposedly dominated by the media it was important to see what effect this had had on the Christian journeys of the participants.

They were first asked about what they remembered doing from their childhood and teens.

38% mentioned reading Christian books (other than the Bible)
39% mentioned watching Christian films and TV programmes
31% mentioned watching Christian plays and musicals

Many had experienced all, but a third had come across none. For some the effect had been considerable — far more so than the effect of the many years of schooling.

It was noticeable that participants aged 25 and under were much more likely to have read Christian books and those aged 35 and under were more likely to have watched Christian plays and musicals than older people.

The press and the electronic media

When asked what they remembered from childhood nobody mentioned any newspaper or magazine article. TV programmes such as *Songs of Praise* were mentioned occasionally but there was little sense that they had made a deep impression with the exception of this Anglican woman of 38 describing herself when she was a teenager:

> *"I would try and watch films about Jesus because I wanted to know more about him. My family didn't love me and I got comfort through watching these films, but I had to be careful that my parents didn't find out. When I watched these films I got a warm glow inside me: I wanted to know more but I didn't know who to ask . . . I wanted to be loved so much by Jesus but my family condemned him."*

An exception was the film *Jesus of Nazareth* (starring Robert Powell) which had made some people revise their ideas:

"It started to stir something in me which showed that Jesus was more than just the Son of God but someone who you could relate to personally; I couldn't believe something so horrible could happen to such a man."

But these are rare exceptions. TV is a cool medium. People watch it in the privacy of their homes — there is not the same sense of occasion as an outing to the cinema or theatre. It is also possible that TV programmes are watched with less concentration: the viewer has to cope with commercial breaks . . . the phone going . . . the cat needing to be let out of the room. TV seldom grips the centre of someone's being.

Participants were asked also about the effect that the media had in their adult journey to faith.

Many Christians feel concerned that the church should be doing more where the media is concerned or we shall let the devil have all the best tunes. The responses suggested we need not be over-anxious about this. Nobody mentioned a Christian TV or radio programme as the main factor in their coming to faith. Only 6% said these had been some supporting influence, like the young woman who had been watching a baptism on *Songs of Praise* on the television and a friend asked her if she wanted to be baptized herself, or an Anglican who was helped by *The Hour of the Power*, an American religious programme on satellite TV.

The effect of the electronic media upon adults seems to be no greater than it is among youngsters. Obviously it can be argued that if the amount of Christian broadcasting was as great as in the United States the effect might be greater, but there is little evidence to show that that would inevitably be so. Research in the United States shows that even their non–stop high profile religious TV and radio has little impact on non–Christians. It plays mainly to its own audience, who tend to be blue collar Christians. Despite the claims which are sometimes made for the evangelistic impact of Christian radio and TV stations there is little evidence in this survey that they lead to many in England finding God and being incorporated into their local churches — though their impact in other parts of the world may well be different.

Literature, drama, and music

The books which affected people when they were young were often stories of missionaries or of persecuted Christians and such people as St Bernadette and Joan of Arc. *The Imitation of Christ* (Thomas à Kempis) was one of the few classics which had an impact. The most influential books seem to be the writings of C. S. Lewis:

> *"I was interested in morals and ethics and read some of C. S.*
> *Lewis's essays. I was intellectually interested and went on to read*
> *other library books on Christian ethics . . . I then began to read the*
> *Bible . . ."* (Anglican male teacher of 35.)

The Cross and the Switchblade, the story of Nicky Cruz by David
Wilkerson (Marshall Pickering, 1964) and the Nicky Cruz books are
mentioned by several people.

> *"At 16 I read* The Cross and the Switchblade *— I was very*
> *impressed by the way in which things had 'come together' in his*
> *life — for me it made Christianity relevant to the real world."*
> (Catholic Income Tax Officer of 33.)

Surprising things surfaced. The epics of Cecil B de Mille were mentioned often — *The Ten Commandments* seems to have made a particular impression, and even *Samson and Delilah* gets a mention.

> *"Something that had seemed so old fashioned and dead came alive*
> *to me."*

> *"The Ten Commandments created a lot of new feelings that still*
> *remain (34 years later)."*

It was noteworthy that films and books were mentioned far more frequently than TV programmes.

The musicals *Jesus Christ Superstar* and *Godspell* had considerable
impact on some — "the first time it struck me that there is life, joy,
sadness in Christianity: that Jesus might really have been a man."

Some people saw these as both direct and indirect causes of their
turning to God.

> *"Jesus Christ Superstar set me back on the road to Christianity — it*
> *seemed as though Christianity came out of the closet."*

The effect of such material as the Hollywood biblical epics and such shows as
Godspell and *Jesus Christ Superstar* highlights the importance of the Christian
community being aware of their impact. It should try to make it commercially
viable for films and shows which portray the Bible and stories of outstanding
Christian men and women to be shown in local cinemas and theatres. It may
be that the church will need to look at the importance of such films and shows
— possibly providing venues in which they can be shown if it is impossible to
encourage cinemas to show them.

When we went on to ask about the influence of Christian literature,
drama, and music upon their recent past 2% said it was the main factor in their coming to faith and 16% said it had played an important
supporting role. Roman Catholics were particularly helped by these

means — for them the figures were 3% and 27%.

Particularly striking was the difference between the effects of the electronic media (TV and radio) and the "live" — books read, cinemas, theatres, and concert halls visited.

Although the amount of time most people are exposed to books and live plays and music during the week is far less than the number of hours they are exposed to TV and radio the effect was considerably greater.

"I visited Coventry Cathedral and was moved by its story." (Baptist man of 45.)

"I told God there was no way I was going to spend my life searching for him — I didn't want to go through the Jehovah's Witness thing again. The answer came quite quickly. I read Mere Christianity *by C. S. Lewis and this was a revelation to me — it seemed too good to be true. I did some reading about other religions and secular philosophies but it seemed to me that Jesus was the greatest revelation of God to man . . . I committed my life to Christ."* (Young Catholic student.)

Not surprisingly, given the nature of the survey, participants tended to concentrate on media which could be labelled "religious". However the constant exposure to the "non–religious" media will inevitably have had an effect on them as upon all of us.

There were a few stories of people who had been touched by things other than "Christian" literature etc. A Roman Catholic research historian encountered Christ through his work:

"I found myself coming across the Christian aspect of the arts (including art and architecture). Gradual immersion in all these made me realize there's something more important underlying it."

An Anglican accountant said:

"I read a couple of books on Near Death Experiences. The Bible came out in paperback about the same time and I bought one out of curiosity having had my interest stirred by the books on NDEs. I was very shaken to find similarities . . . and started going to a local church to find out more."

This survey suggests that if the church wishes to evangelize through the media, the electronic means are less effective than others. Support should therefore be given to live drama, literature and music at least as much as to TV and radio.

Some churches channel their resources towards electronic rather than "live" presentations: the survey suggests this may be a mistake. The size of audience for the "live" may be only a tiny fraction of that for the electronic media but it appears to have a greater effect.

CHAPTER 8

Evangelistic events

In the popular stereotype, evangelism is big events, and to evangelize is to organize big events. This research shows conclusively that this is certainly not the only or even the main way to evangelize. This is not a new finding: research done independently by Gavin Reid, John Finney, and the Methodist Church in the 1980s gave figures of 13%, 11%, and 5% respectively (slightly different questions may account for some of the differences).

When we asked about the importance of these events at the time that participants turned to God there was little difference between men and women.

On average:

4% said it was the main factor
13% said it was a supporting factor

Billy Graham was mentioned more than all the other evangelists put together, but Nicky Cruz also made an impact. He is mentioned favourably by a number of people including one man who could not understand what he was saying because of his thick accent!

There were pronounced differences between denominations. About a third of Baptist and 25% of New Church participants said these events had either a main or a supporting role in their journey to faith — compared with 13% of Anglicans and 4% of Roman Catholics.

The evidence for the value of evangelistic events is difficult to analyze. At first glance it looks as though they have a definite but fairly limited effect — for a minority they are highly significant while having a neutral or negative effect on others.

On the other hand participation in such events may encourage Christians to be more outgoing in their relations with others and so have an effect which is not directly recorded. Further, churches taking part in missions may improve their morale and so their members may be more ready to invite others to join.

At the same time the low percentage of participants attributing value to these events has to be taken seriously. The research covered a period which was a few years after the major Billy Graham (1984 and

1985) and Luis Palau (London 1983–84) events and these were mentioned by some as a memorable incident which helped them to consider the Christian faith. Some in the survey had found faith at these meetings.

A third of all participants mentioned that they had been taken to rallies with Christian speakers while they were young — Billy Graham and the Pope were most frequently mentioned.

The effect of the big rallies was very varied. For some it was the time when they turned to God — like this Anglican woman of 39 remembering herself as a youngster:

> " . . .I found myself going down to the front and crying. When I got to the bottom of the church I fell to my knees . . . Jesus had his hand on me all these years."

Others however felt they were too young and had not understood what was happening. Some saw the events as negative. A woman of 44 said:

> "I listened to the preachers saying 'You are a sinner'. It had the same effect on me at 10 as being told 'you're not worth anything'. Just when self-confidence is building up — it stopped mine completely."

and a Salvation Army art student said:

> "At Luis Palau rallies I was often overwhelmed by the power and presence of the meeting, yet sadly I often found my response to this was based more on emotion and I was often left confused with poor and very little follow-up from counsellors."

Others were neutral, like a Baptist teacher of 44 remembering his early days:

> "They were just outings to me."

But another Baptist said:

> "I went forward at a Luis Palau 'Mission to London' meeting to voice my commitment . . . I became more determined to sort this Christianity thing out for myself."

There is certainly a good deal of evidence that children have mixed reactions to big meetings. A Roman Catholic recalled that going as a youngster to a "Pentecostal 'thing' frightened me to death". A 48–year–old Methodist remembered being taken to conventions and how "the intense emotion of these gatherings affected me strongly, but in my late teens I secretly resented having to give up leisure activities to attend these gatherings." A 16–year–old Anglican, who had been greatly helped by books by Nicky Cruz and Jackie Pullinger (*Chasing the Dragon* by Pullinger and Quicke, Hodder and Stoughton, 1980) found Christian rallies:

> " . . . *quite embarrassing really and found them a bit false
> sometimes, though I have seen amazing things done at some of
> these. It just wasn't really amazing for me and didn't help me
> much.*"

But there were many who had found a very real faith at major rallies.

> "*I was sitting listening to Billy Graham . . . I felt an inner tugging
> to go to the front and there gave my heart to the Lord.*" (Young
> Baptist computer operator.)

> "*It was at a Salvation Army event that I decided to commit myself
> to God. I had to go the front for this . . .*" (Young female
> accountant.)

> "*He was preaching about becoming a Christian. I was very
> interested in this and he had a little booklet you could buy for five
> pence. On the back was a prayer you could pray to become a
> Christian.*" (Young Methodist student.)

It might be expected that evangelistic events are primarily for the
(comparatively small) group of people who have "sudden" conversions.
But those who have a more gradual experience also find them helpful.
This Baptist woman's story shows the part which the big event played
for her in the ladder of experiences which led her upwards to God:

> "*I sometimes attended my daughter's church and found a sense of
> peace and love . . .*
> *gradually I made enquiries through a Christian friend at work and
> she invited me to see Billy Graham . . .*
> *I went forward and asked Jesus Christ to come into my life . . .*
> *I began going to my local church and took study lessons . . .*
> *my life is gradually changing.*"

OTHER EVANGELISTIC EVENTS

Baptism

A service which is certainly evangelistic though not always recognized
as such is baptism. A number had found that the baptism of someone
else was their own way into faith. For many it was the baptism of their
child, but in this case it was not the service itself which was evangelistic but the personal relationships the family made with the minister,
and the preparation which they were asked to do beforehand.

Where adults were being baptized it was the actual service which evangelized:

"After my sister–in–law's baptism my husband and I came away feeling that we needed to go to church . . . during that service what the minister was saying seemed as if it was all for us. After the service was over my husband went and saw the minister and it was at this time that we realized that we wanted the Lord into our lives and that was the 5th of November. It was really a wonderful feeling, it was amazing." (43–year–old Baptist sales assistant.)

A student said simply:

"I went to her baptism and gave my life to the Lord."

The full potential of adult baptism services as an opportunity for evangelizing should be realized. It was noticeable that neither baptism services for children nor confirmation services were mentioned by anybody as directly evangelistic. Those churches which practise infant baptism and confirmation may need to make more effective use of these opportunities.

The Eucharist

It was also noticeable that for a lesser number the Eucharist had been a turning point:

"I heard that a very close friend had been killed suddenly. For two days I walked around kicking the walls. Then I went to a family service and when I went forward for communion I suddenly felt at peace and knew it was all right . . . I had never been to a communion rail before in my life and at that time I did not actually take communion but I did take a blessing." (47–year–old Methodist man.)

"For five years I had been reading the Bible quite regularly. The pop group U2 led me to find answers in the Christian faith. Early 1990 I wanted to return to church. A friend introduced me to a lay pastor. Through his invitation I went to church. When it came to receiving Holy Communion he asked 'Do you know Jesus Christ as your Lord and Saviour?' At that point I knew I did, so went up to receive communion." (36–year–old Methodist woman.)

"After communion I asked for forgiveness. I could not eat or drink — the bread and the wine they stuck in my throat. So I spoke to someone at church who said 'God has been speaking to you'. I was

*so confused — gob–smacked! My best friend talked with me the
next day."* (42–year–old man from a New Church.)

*"I was on a one day retreat at the home of priests. In the chapel, at
the end of the day, mass was held. The theme, forgiveness, was
deeply inspirational. Father Jim celebrated mass with my friends
and family standing around the altar — and he explained the
sharing of the eucharist in terms of the Last Supper. I realized then
that the forgiveness and healing I needed was in the eucharist. I
then decided to become a Catholic."* (40–year–old man.)

Other events

Some "happenings" were evangelistic although they were not directly
linked with a church. A Baptist woman experienced a meeting of those
who have a problem with alcohol:

*"I attended Al Anon meetings with my mother who is an alcoholic
. . . I was influenced by a lady who became a Christian through Al
Anon. She attended church and I saw a great difference in her life.
She was calmer and didn't gossip any more. She gave up drinking
and smoking and illegal receiving of stolen goods and getting
money by deception . . ."*

CHAPTER 9

Is there a change?

It was important to find out what had happened as a result of the "turning to God". Was it a formality which led to no perceptible alteration of behaviour? <u>Was it life–changing</u>?

Questions were asked about the obviously "religious" side of the life of the participants in order to see what changes had occurred. But a change in religious behaviour should only be a surface indicator of a much deeper change that faith has bought. In order to discover the wider changes of attitude or behaviour which had taken place, <u>we asked participants how they felt that they themselves had altered. We also asked if other people had commented on how they had changed</u> — though we did not, of course, have the opportunity of interviewing these people.

As might be expected people prayed more, went to church more, and read the Bible more. While becoming a Christian is much more than religious observances of this kind; they are useful markers of the change in the level of commitment which has taken place.

GOING TO CHURCH

There were clearly a minority for whom the "public profession of faith" had been part of their churchgoing career. They had been attending regularly and this was a further step.

But this was far from typical. Figure 18 shows that for nearly 70% who had previously only gone occasionally if at all the step made an enormous difference. For these adults their Christian faith had meant a considerable change in their way of life. At the most obvious level it meant that the car would have to get washed at another time than Sunday morning, the children would have to be arranged for, Sunday lunch might have to be at a different time, there could be no Sunday morning lie–in (spoken of with feeling by quite a number!). It was also clear from other replies that much deeper changes in their attitude to other people, their view of themselves and the world around them had happened.

73

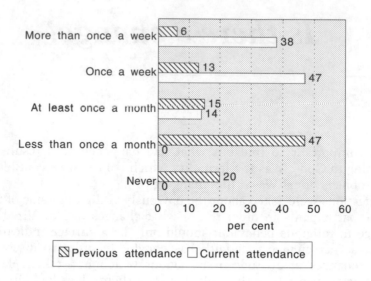

Fig. 18 Frequency of church attendance.

Moreover, over a third now <u>attend church</u> more than once a week
with men being more likely than women to go more than once a week
— possibly because women more frequently cited household responsi-
bilities as a hindrance.

Many were involved in groups of one kind or another. 49% went to
a <u>house group</u> or other church organization at least once a week and a
further 23% went at least once a month. These were obviously a major
part of the ongoing support they received after the teaching they had
received in preparation for their public profession. It may be a matter
of some concern that despite the very high level of satisfaction which
we shall find is recorded for the preparation phase a considerable number now had no ongoing support apart from Sunday worship.
Sometimes this is for reasons which may not be immediately obvious
for it is clear that not all found it easy to join a group or organization:

*"I am afraid to join a house group since I am a poor reader — silly
reason but true."*

*"I would like to become more involved but I feel as though I am
not well enough educated."*

*"I would like to be more involved, to be more like them, but I don't
think it is in my nature."*

Many groups and organizations tend to assume a certain type of educational background: people often read the Bible — sometimes reading it aloud, they study explanatory material and then discuss it. Groups and organizations can get an elitist reputation in a church and the last two quotations above clearly felt that they did not come up to the required standard.

Not all feel comfortable with the "normal" methodology of a group — and these can include the unexpected: the person who confessed to being a poor reader is an aeronautical engineer. There is need for material to be produced which is not dependant so much on the written word but more on relationships, visual material, and methods of prayer in which anyone can join. This in turn requires better training for those who are leading the groups and organizations.

Obstacle course?

Did people find the transition to churchgoing difficult? The idea, which is widely held within the church, that beginning to go to church is a difficult operation is only partially borne out by the research.

We asked "How easy or difficult did you find it to start going more regularly?" The answers varied considerably depending as to whether or not there had been any previous history of churchgoing:

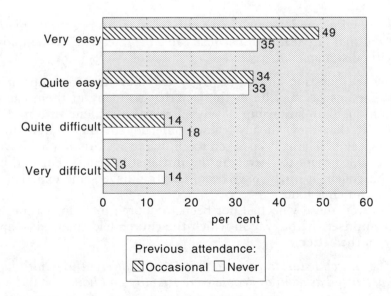

Fig. 19 Ease/difficulty of regular church attendance.

First of all the responses of the 80% in the survey who had some previous experience of going to church as an adult.

The occasional churchgoers

How easy had they found going to church more regularly?

There seemed to be no difference between rural or urban churches, between different parts of the country or different socio–economic groups. The main distinction is that women found it markedly more difficult to begin going to church regularly than men: 19% found it quite or very difficult compared with 11% of men. Possibly this is because of family pressures or less self–confidence.

Of course we were asking those who had successfully managed to get inside the church. There will certainly be those who are turned away because they find entering the "church culture" too daunting: research into this is needed.

> *"Vicar encouraged children — have not found many vicars that do."* (Anglican school dinner lady.)

> *"I sat next to an old lady: she welcomed me to the church and I felt at home."* (Anglican student of 17.)

> *"Church is fun and the stereotype of old, dark and dreary buildings needs to be changed."* (Baptist man of 47.)

> *"I enjoy the handclapping and seeing the teenagers getting involved — not that I do it myself because I'm a bit reserved."* (Unemployed Methodist man.)

Maybe the question should be: Why did they find it comparatively easy. The answer may lie in the fact that so many of them came to faith through a relationship — with a relative, a friend or a minister. They felt that they already knew somebody in the church. Indeed many speak of having been taken to church by a Christian, who would have enabled them to overcome the initial strangeness. Further, however infrequent it might have been, they did have some experience of what a church is like.

However, those who had not been to church for a long time were often surprised by the way in which the church had changed — apparently for the better:

> *"The church I started going to was so very different to what I had experienced as a child. People were friendly and honest, children were welcomed, and there was a great emphasis on 'community'."* (29–year–old Catholic.)

"The services were friendly and enjoyable. It wasn't miserable stuff, which a lot of church services used to be." (Anglican man of 60.)

They were also asked *why* they started to go more regularly. Obviously the "right" answer would be "to worship God", but only 36% put a spiritual need in so many words — "to learn about God", "meet with Jesus", to "feed my faith". 27% said they wanted or needed to go without saying why. 34% mentioned social needs — fellowship, taking the children and so on. Only 2% said that they went to church to receive the sacrament. As might have been expected the reasons why people go to church are very varied indeed and further research needs to be done on this.

The non-churchgoers

We were particularly interested in those who said that they had never previously gone to church. These were 24% of the men and 17% of the women. Their adult lifestyle had never included churchgoing. If the church is to have impact in this country it must seek to touch those who have no experience of the Christian church and virtually no knowledge of its message. It has been suggested elsewhere (see *The Church on the Move* by John Finney, DLT, 1992) that these may be almost half the total population — and it is a growing proportion as a generation of children grows up which has never had any contact with a Christian church.

First of all it was encouraging that 84 of our participants fell into this category — about half of whom had had some experience of the church as children. Had they been able to make the change?

We found that these 84 were even more addicted to churchgoing than those who had some previous experience: 92% went at least once a week (only 80% of the others were so regular).

But how easy had it been for them? The figures are markedly different from those who had had some previous adult experience of the church (see Fig. 19 on page 75). When they are compared with those above it is clear that if people have been to church, even if it is only very occasionally, it makes it much easier for them to start going more regularly. The 32% of previous non-churchgoers who found it difficult are a matter for real concern.

"We found a 'them' and 'us' situation and we didn't know anyone. It wasn't until we went along to one or two social events that we felt more relaxed." (46-year-old Anglican male accountant.)

"I didn't feel my way around the service. It was a mechanical exercise, and I used to worry about getting things wrong." (Anglican woman psychologist.)

"I felt weird the first Sunday back. I found it difficult to walk in but the church secretary gave me an enormous smile at the door and from then on I felt good inside." (Male Baptist insurance supervisor of 34.)

"I'd got used to lying around in bed. A lot of words I didn't understand. I felt a bit of a failure." (16–year–old in an ecumenical church.)

"I was afraid of being an obvious learner." (Retired Anglican woman.)

"When you walk into our church the people don't really know how to make you welcome." (Anglican housewife.)

This comment from an Anglican teacher sums up the feelings of many:

"However welcome one is made to feel, the service and people are not within one's normal sphere. Also, purely changing routine and 'making time' requires effort."

This honest comment also deserves to be included:

"I was a very vociferous atheist. I was worried about who'd see me in church and say 'Aha!'." (Woman of 43.)

Churches have to take these "human" aspects into consideration, for they are the things which hold many back. Evangelism is too spiritual if it ignores them.

It was also noticeable that these people without a church background often felt themselves to be not yet accepted into the full life of their church. 41% of them (compared with 28% of the occasional churchgoers) described themselves as "not very" or "not at all" involved. This is despite the fact that they go to church more than the "occasionals". In other words many of these people still feel themselves to be on the outside of their church.

It is not easy to put oneself into the shoes of someone who has *never* been to church before. Churches need to look at themselves from the point of view of a complete outsider and make sure they are user–friendly. Some churches have found that they can get this viewpoint if they ask two people who have never been to their church before to go to a service and report honestly on their reactions.

We also asked them why they started to attend: the reasons are worth setting out in detail:

To learn/out of curiosity	14%
I became a Christian	11%
In search of God	5%
To worship God	5%
To feed my faith	3%
I wanted to	13%
I was invited by friends/relatives	11%
To take the children	10%
I was invited by the minister	5%
Fellowship	13%

Their motivation was markedly different from those who had been to church occasionally before. The need for fellowship was much less obvious — understandably so since they were not yet likely to know many people in the congregation. People who had never been to church were far more likely to mention being invited by someone, and they were more likely to find that taking their children was a motive. If there is nobody to go with (even if it is your own child) entering a church is a difficult operation for those who have never been.

Training in evangelization should mention that one of the simplest and most effective forms of evangelism is, "Would you like to come along with me to church next Sunday?".

This presupposes that the church member giving the invitation feels confident that the church will welcome their friend.

Which church did these people choose when they decided to go?

43% went to the one recommended by their friends (suggestions could be of all kinds — "the lady in the registry office recommended URC for marrying divorcees."

11% went to one where they knew the minister.

17% went to the nearest church — "it was the first church I came to."

8% searched for one they liked — "we went to three churches in the area and liked the worship best at the one we go to now — also, the welcome we received there had quite a big influence."

5% had a sense of being led by God.

17% gave other answers.

A few have a robust attitude to getting into the life of the church:

"I felt that it is God's home and now I've stood up and professed to be a Christian I've got a damn good right to be here. I say that

because there are some at church (older) who claim to have been
Christians for years and tend to regard the newcomers as
intruders." (Anglican ward receptionist of 36.)

But not all have such a forthright attitude — this is far more typical:

"I was quite shy at the time and I found it difficult to walk in —
what should I be doing now?" (Methodist woman of 29.)

Perhaps surprisingly there seemed to be hardly any denominational differences. It was as difficult — or as easy — to become part of any.

Denominational fluidity

It has often been remarked that there is far less denominational loyalty
than used to be the case. This survey confirmed this. Indeed about one
in ten saw themselves as belonging to more than one denomination.

There was naturally a tendency for people to remain in the same
denomination as the one in which they were brought up. But there is
far more change than is often supposed.

There was no difference in fluidity between those going to rural and
those going to urban churches despite the greater "availability" of different denominations in the towns and cities.

The "fluidity factor" varies markedly from denomination to denomination. Some participants had changed their denomination before the
period of turning to God but, as might be expected, the likelihood of
transfer increased during the period of spiritual change when they were
asking new questions and looking for support. No less than 20% had
changed their denomination during or since this period, and a further
7% had changed the church they went to (though remaining in the
same denomination). Some of the reasons they gave for the change
were straightforward — they moved house, or wanted to go to the
same church as their partner.

Often, however they changed because they preferred the style of
worship at the other church. Their views about the churches they have
left are predictably trenchant:

"I am the only member of the youth group at the URC and feel I
am missing out on fellowship. I feel I would like to go to a more
charismatic church." (Girl moving into a Baptist church.)

"We felt there was something lacking. We wanted more of the Word
and more teaching and deeper relationships, and to see the body
moving in the gifts." (Retired man who is now Methodist —
formerly Anglican.)

"I changed because of the attitude of the Catholics: i.e. you can do or say anything as long as you go to confession." (Hospital caterer now an Anglican.)

"The Anglican church was a waste of time and did not relate to modern society — also that it was poorly led and was not going anywhere." (Chartered surveyor now a Catholic.)

"Leadership were threatened by any questioning of doctrine and I could no longer trust them." (Doctor — formerly New Church, now an Anglican.)

"I found the C. of E. services very dull and uninspiring. My current church is more friendly and the services are more meaningful." (Woman building surveyor who is now URC.)

"I think I would have been Catholic from the beginning if I'd been introduced to it then, but I was put off by evangelical Christians and am still regarded as needing to be rescued by some of them. It's very sad." (50–year–old piano teacher.)

"Husband divorced me and made situation embarrassing to remain within Catholic faith." (34–year–old dinner lady.)

It is difficult to make generalizations but on the whole the movement has been towards the churches which are more charismatic and freer in their workship.

The church which produces the most varied opinions is the Church of England. Some found it thoroughly offputting — dreariness is the most common complaint — and left for another denomination. Others are extremely enthusiastic: on the whole it is the Anglican churches which seemed to be most "open" in their worship and fellowship which attract.

The overall picture is of a highly mobile and rather "choosey" clientele. They have begun their journey of faith within a certain denomination and with a certain group of friends but they do not feel themselves committed. They look for an appropriate fellowship through which their faith can be worked out. They have made considerable sacrifices in terms of changing their lifestyle to follow Christ and they expect to be part of a church which will help them, and be congenial. They are understandably unwilling to put up with what they see as second best. It is not good enough for churches to say, "they must take us as we are", when their style is unhelpful to those coming into the Christian faith.

Churches may need to undertake the painful task of seeing if any new people have left them and gone elsewhere. Finding out the reasons by talking with the people concerned and putting the lessons learnt into effect could be very salutary.

READING THE BIBLE

We have already looked at the amount of Bible–reading that people did during the time when they were becoming Christians, and we found that while only 5% said it was the main factor in their becoming Christians a quarter of them saw it as an important supporting factor in the process.

When they were asked about the amount of Bible reading people did now — a year or so after their public profession we found that there was very little change.

- Those who read the Bible "several times a week" went up from 47% to 54%
- Those who read the Bible "several times a month" went down from 13% to 11%.
- Those who read the Bible "occasionally" went up from 21% to 25%
- The most significant change was that those who read the Bible "seldom or never" went down from 19% to 10%.

It was clear that the Bible was still a significant support to their spiritual life: 62% said it was "very important" to them and 29% said it was "quite important".

A comparison of the two sets of responses shows that although 91% said it was important to them, almost half did not read it all that regularly. 36% of them read it at best only "several times a month" and 10% seldom or never read it.

THE IMAGE OF GOD

The Christian faith is based upon trust in God through Christ. Each of us have an "icon" of God — an image which for the present represents God to us. The Bible itself speaks of Christ as the eikon of God — as we see him so we see the Father. But this perception may take many forms

- Some see him in pictorial terms: as an old man with a beard, for example.
- Some see him semi–pictorially: as light or beauty.
- Some, possibly most, see God as a collection of adjectives: those attributes which seem to be part of the character of God: loving, powerful, just, caring, etc.

To discover someone's relationship with God it is often helpful to find out what "icon" they have and whether it is sharp and precise or vague, distant, and hazy.

It was therefore important to discover how far our participants had changed their view of God as a result of their "turning". Not wishing to put suggestions in their minds they were asked two open–ended questions:

"How would you have described God before . . .?"

"How would you describe him now?

The questions were seen to be important — over three–quarters answered these far from straightforward queries.

The results were clear.

Only 13% of people said that their view of God had *not* changed.

It was noticeable that people were much more enthusiastic about describing the God they know now than in describing the "icon" they had previously.

Once again it is clear that most of these people had some sort of belief in God. In post–Christian England people have not become atheists — only 7% in this sample claimed to have been non–believers, although the temptation must have been to over–emphasize the difference between "before" and "after" for dramatic purposes. (It says much for the integrity of the people taking part in the survey that there is no sense of writing a "good story" — indeed some apologized for not having a more melodramatic testimony to tell.)

The descriptions which participants used were (some used more than one):

	BEFORE	AFTER
• Does not exist/very doubtful "old–fashioned, boring, probably non–existent" "Non–existent? Possibly? I hated him! I'm not really sure."	7%	—
• Stern, judgemental, harsh "frightened of him — strict, stern, Victorian father" " . . .someone like a headmaster" "someone who stopped you from doing what you wanted"	9%	1%
• Remote, unapproachable, irrelevant "someone on another plane, who wasn't really connected at all" "God was an antique . . .out of date" "you couldn't pray to him directly — had to go through the Virgin Mary and the saints — very distant"	24%	1%
• Old man in the sky "a big bubbly man with a big white beard" "Super Santa Claus"	12%	—

	BEFORE	AFTER
• For use in emergencies	6%	1%
• A generalized force or spirit "unpredictable . . .where people go when they die: when my Grandad died I was told 'he's gone to see Jesus'"	6%	3%
• Mighty, wonderful "someone with a bleeding heart for the world"	8%	14%
• Creator/power that sustains the universe	12%	17%
• Just	—	3%
• Friend/always with me/someone to talk to "someone to run to" "He's yearning to love me and to listen to me and help me."	13%	(63%)
• Father "someone I can talk to" "someone I respect and love"	4%	(22%)

However, the masculine analogy was not found helpful
by some:
"God is not a he or she any more. S/he has lost this
vengefulness and has become a partner to whom I can
talk . . ."
"I am still learning to trust him — the 'male' father
figure draws out anger."
"not necessarily male — young, up with the times, and
someone who knows what's going on in the world"

	BEFORE	AFTER
• Guide	1%	8%
• Loving/kind/forgiving "He is beautiful. When I think about him it makes me feel happy: he's always doing surprises for me."	9%	(46%)

There is a shift from:
   the pictorial or semi–pictorial to the "attribute centred" view
   the vague to the more precise
   the impersonal to the personal
   the distant to the intimate
   the irrelevant to the contemporary

Changes in the way in which people regard God are taking place throughout their lives and an important part of evangelism must be the encouraging of a more authentic and adult view of God.

This is especially true of a time of "turning". This is not necessarily subsequent to the change — brought about by teaching and the personal experience of God as a practising Christian. It is likely that the change in the "icon" takes place, at least in part, before the turning takes place — indeed before it is able to take place. After all few people would wish to commit themselves to a God who they envisaged as Father Christmas, or as a Victorian domestic tyrant.

A major part of evangelism therefore is to help people to develop an "icon" of God which is richer and fuller, more biblical, and more relevant to themselves. This may well mean that they need to change the image which they had. The most important emphases needed at this point in their spiritual lives seem to be that God is a person, is relevant, and is friendly.

It certainly calls into question the preaching of a God of wrath who coldly demands obedience. Such emphasis on one aspect of the holiness of God means that the more personal elements are secondary. Such teaching merely reinforces the stern, repressive image that many people have and may well be counter–productive in an age when few have any other view of God which could counterbalance it. This 38–year–old teacher from a New Church describes her journey into the love of God:

> "While I was with the [Jehovah's] Witnesses God was harsh and judgemental and vengeful. After being with the URC God was not as bad as that but certainly more distant than now . . . even though I was aware that God must be a God of love. Now I feel as though I've got closer . . ."

Some might wish to say that the participants have gone too far in seeing God in such immanent and personal terms, and the view of the cosmic God is largely missing as is any emphasis on the perfection and purity of God (the word "holiness" was very seldom used), or God's demand for justice and integrity in the social order, and in creation.

It is very difficult to generalize but it is likely that people's apprehension of God passes through three stages:

1. God is seen as a vague "otherness". If there is any more concrete image it is of a Father — either of the Santa Claus variety or of a heavenly bookkeeper keeping track of sins.
2. The personal breaks through and people respond by loving God themselves. He is seen as the ideal, portrayed particularly in Jesus. For this reason, among others, the cross of Christ is important in showing the depth of God's love and the offer of forgiveness for those who are conscious of guilt. At this stage a warm sense of God as personal saviour and friend is uppermost.
3. The idea of God as creator and redeemer of the world becomes included in the individual's thinking. On the one hand there will be such concepts as the transcendent Christ who holds history in his hand, and on the other the immanent God seen suffering in the oppressed and in care for this planet. These wider views become integrated into the image of God as a close friend. Not surprisingly, because the participants had only just made a profession of faith, this element was not dominant in the survey.

In Christian teaching for those who have little knowledge of the faith it is probably the second stage which should be stressed. The love of God in Christ should be presented in such a way as to show God as someone who could be a personal friend and guide who can make sense of our lives. To jump straight to the third stage is unlikely to answer the questions about personal relevance, though there will need to be some allusion to this area in order to show that there is more to the Christian faith than an I–thou relationship. (This present research needs to be put alongside the work on faith formation which has already been done by Fowler, Westerhof, etc.)

One wider question presented itself to some: the move from the first to second stage brings into sharper focus the problem of suffering. If God is seen as remote and uninterested in the world then suffering is not directly his "fault". When he is seen as a friend and guide the problem becomes more acute. This story puts it clearly:

> *"A few weeks ago I was very upset. A Christian lady in the church was dying of cancer. Her husband was a Christian too. She wanted to die before him — but he died suddenly in his sleep. She was left alone so she threw herself into the river and drowned. You profess to believe that God is your friend; but why does he allow things to happen? We should be asking questions. God wants us to question."* (Unemployed Methodist man of 53.)

The questions posed by a suffering world are bound to arise as soon as people begin to think of God in more personal and contemporaneous terms. It is an important area and any evangelistic approach should be prepared to tackle it squarely.

Those who evangelize must take seriously the importance of the changing image of God that most people coming to faith will be encountering. Teaching and preaching therefore should be about God not just our response to God.

The request many people seem to be making is "Show us the Father."

THE CONTENT OF BELIEF

It could easily be assumed that turning to God would sort out people's intellectual uncertainties for them. On the contrary the survey shows that coming to faith seemed to leave as many questions afterwards as people had before. It was good to see that a profession of faith did not mean that minds were closed.

60% of people said they had no difficulties about the Christian message either before or after turning to God, with the ABC1s having rather more difficulties than the C2DEs and the Methodists having more than the Baptists. But of the large minority that did have uncertainties:

5% had problems with	Genesis and creation	beforehand	and 3% after
2%	the Old Testament		4%
3%	the Virgin Birth		2%
1%	the book of Revelation		2%
2%	life after death		2%

Belief in the resurrection is the only exception to this very equal level of doubt, and not by much: 6% doubted it before, and 2% afterwards — all of them ABC1s!

As people began to read their Bible closely, difficulties emerged, especially in the Old Testament:

"I started reading Genesis and I found it hard to come to terms with people being 600 years old . . . the cruelness in some of the passages — you have this picture of what the Bible should be — the reality of it shocks you." (43–year–old Baptist sales assistant.)

"I still believe that the bits about the way the earth was created is codswallop. Also where it says people lived 700 years." (Anglican woman of 23.)

An Anglican production line manager could put the problems on one side, but he was in a small minority:

"I have been trained as a scientist — I sometimes find it difficult to believe in anything which cannot be proved. I try to circumvent this by not considering it. I am patient enough to wait for an answer."

Once again it has to be remembered that the people being interviewed had recently been through some sort of "induction course" into the Christian faith. Clearly many of their questions still remained. Indeed it may be that the course had made it difficult for them to raise the issues again since they were supposed to have been dealt with.

People need help in understanding the content of their faith *after* their public profession as well as before.

It may need to be on a fairly elementary level — a lot of the comments were about Adam and Eve, violence in the Old Testament, Methuselah, and the book of Revelation ("If God's such a nice chap, why would he have so many folk praising him. It must be very embarrassing for him"). Help is needed on the right way to read these passages, because often it was not difficulties about belief which were being mentioned but of biblical interpretation. A more complex subject raised by some is the position of women in the church and the Bible.

Not many said that they had been faced with major ethical questions. One or two people said they had found that their faith, "clashed with what I wanted to do . . . I found the teaching on sexual behaviour and marriage difficult to take."

It had been hoped that the research would discover those parts of the Christian message which were particularly appealing to different groups of people. It is unlikely for example that a professional man with no worries is helped by the same part of the faith as a pensioner grieving for her husband. However the answers were given in such general terms that it was unsafe to draw conclusions. Forgiveness and the love of God were the most frequently mentioned. More research needs to be done in this area.

The participants' own view of the change

The Christian life is obviously much more than going to Church, reading the Bible, and thinking more about God. The difference which their turn to God had made in the way they lived their lives and how this change was perceived by others was at least as important. Once again we used open–ended questions to probe how the participants thought the change had affected them.

Overwhelmingly those in the survey felt that becoming a Christian had been a "good thing". There is a stream of testimonies to the fact that they now feel better people:

"I'm not afraid of facing anything."

"It's given life a point." (This sense of having a new purpose in life was particularly common among ABC1s)

"I'm more thoughtful, caring, tolerant, contented, aware of other's needs."

"Never thought I'd be able to forgive people."

"I am happier within myself." (C2DEs were more likely to use the word "happier" to describe themselves.)

"I have given up working too hard at the wrong things."

"Everything makes better sense now."

"It's like having a sixth sense — seeing the world through new eyes."

"I am more trustful of people, I don't worry so much about life."

The hundreds of similar statements can be largely summed up in the phrase used by a home economist of 21: "I feel a lot better about myself." The sense of improved self–worth and self–image is impressive. Many seemed to know themselves much better as a result of their experience: "I am more aware of my strengths and weaknesses."

This is much more than a euphoric "I feel good". A high proportion of participants said that they were now better at personal relationships, more caring, more outward looking and more tolerant of others.

"My attitude towards people has changed drastically. I was a very catty person — always the first person to shout my mouth off. Now I'm always trying to make up . . . less moody."

As was found above when the participants were describing their changing image of God there was little consciousness of the social dimension of being a Christian apart from immediate personal relationships. This 25–year–old Catholic quality engineer was an exception:

"It has given me a new perspective on social/political issues."

Surprisingly few spoke about difficulties they had encountered considering that most had been Christians for at least a year or more. When these were mentioned it was with some such comment as, "if you've got any problems you've got someone to turn to".

If these replies are anything to go by everybody should rush to become a Christian. Not a single person even hinted that they wish that they had not made their journey to God.

What others think about it

While it is important to know how people themselves feel about becoming a Christian it is possibly even more important to know what those close to them feel about it. It was not possible to interview these people so we asked what comments our participants had heard from others on the change in their lives. 43% of the people reported nothing and one person said, "It's too embarrassing to quote". The rest produced a rich store of comments.

Of particular importance were how marriage partners responded to the change in their wife or husband. The majority liked what they saw:

"Husband said I looked 16 again."

"My husband said I'm easier to live with, much more supportive."
(though she goes on to say that he gets frustrated when she says, "We'll pray about it").

"More tolerant with your mother–in–law."

"My wife says 'You're more understanding and helpful'."

"You've grown from a scared little girl to a beautiful confident woman."

But not all marriage relationships were sweet: stress between a Christian and his or her partner was mentioned by a small number of participants:

"It has made life harder between me and my husband — he doesn't understand why I need to go to church."

"My wife says I am obsessed with Christianity."

Sometimes time made a difference:

"It made it more difficult at first because my husband realized the change in me . . .his comment was 'You're not the girl I married', but since I've been a Christian for a year — I haven't tried to enforce my beliefs on him. It's not difficult now — he even comes to church occasionally."

But these negative comments were far fewer than those which were appreciative.

Parents were generally pleased:

"You tackle things in a different way and your value system has changed."

"You're not so snappy, you look happier."

There were exceptions:

" 'Bigotry', from my mother who is very anti–church."

Brothers and sisters were generally in favour:

"I'm pleased for you — you look so happy."

"You haven't half changed since you started going to church."

"You're far less critical and quick–tempered."

but sibling rivalry was still present occasionally:

"It proves that you're weird."

Generally speaking the less close people were to the new Christian the more cynical their response was likely to be. The mainly negative comments come from those who are acquaintances:

"You go to church all the time now — it's all church, church, church."

"'Why don't you come down to the pub more often?' (though I do)."

"He's going through a mid–life crisis. You'll get over it soon."

"I hope it's not contagious."

"Old friends I socialize with tell me they don't want to hear any religion."

"That's not you talking — that's the church."

"They've actually called me the vicar."

"You're not the type to be a Christian."

"You're boring and need to let your hair down and have more fun."

"Fancy you going to church!"

However, even in this group there are plenty of positive remarks:

"A friend says she envies the amount of peace I have over things in life."

"Whatever pills he's been taking, I'll have some of those." (after he came back from Easter People at Llandudno in 1991)

"My boss at work said he'd noticed a change in me, 'You're quieter and different but in a nice way'."

"You've blossomed — you're different."

One woman recorded several comments about herself made by different people:

"You have a light in your eyes." "You don't worry like you used to."

"You love God because your voice is gentle when you talk about him."

"You laugh a lot more now."

Some participants were conscious that they had been like the Methodist couple who knew they had been "a bit forceful in our witness at first". They regretted it because it had given others justification for labelling them "Bible–bashers". Others had neglected previous friendships and this had caused resentment.

No one in the survey said that they had suffered serious persecution because of their faith — there had been plenty of barbed comments and cynical remarks but nothing worse than mockery — though this can be hard enough to take if it continues for any length of time.

CHAPTER 10

Religious experiences

While the survey was primarily trying to follow the path of people who had made a profession of Christian faith it brought into the open other experiences. The work of the Alister Hardy Institute had alerted us to the probability of these and participants were asked whether they had had any "out of the way experiences which you would describe as religious in some way". 43% of the people answered "Yes", and nearly two thirds of these had had more than one such experience — 13% said it was fairly commonplace. ABC1s were rather more likely to tell of them than C2DEs (45% compared with 38%) — and their experiences were more likely to be "charismatic", whereas C2DEs were more likely to tell of dreams and healings.

This chapter is one of the most difficult in the book because what is recounted defies classification and the percentages given need to be treated with some caution. The stories stand on their own.

Further they are impossible to check: it is conceivable that people were making them up in order to impress the interviewer. However it can only be said that nowhere else is there even the hint that stories are being fabricated and some of them are so remarkable that they invite disbelief. The general conclusion has to be that, in at least the vast majority of these accounts, this is how the experience seemed to the person concerned: whether they are describing objective reality is of course another matter which it is impossible to prove on this evidence alone.

CHARISMATIC HAPPENINGS

Charismatic phenomena are now well documented and have been described in many books. A number of participants had had an experience which fell into this category and 5% mentioned receiving the gift of tongues.

The infilling of the Holy Spirit

Much controversy has surrounded this experience. Known by Pentecostals and many charismatics as the "Baptism in the Spirit", it has been variously described by others. Those who have experienced it describe it as a setting free of the Holy Spirit in someone's life in order that he or she may worship God more freely and serve him more powerfully in the world.

> *"There was a time of silence in church and I heard my own name called very deeply within me and I knew that God was calling me and I was really scared . . . I then told the team what had happened and they prayed with me and the Holy Spirit came on me and I was filled with this amazing overwhelming love and although I knew I was loved I felt loved . . . that was the start of the call into healing — by entering nursing."* (Evangelical man of 45.)

> *"God filled me with Holy Spirit at a service where preacher spoke about helping the homeless. Tears, laughter, joy, peace. It was three months after I became a Christian."* (Methodist shop manageress of 36.)

> *" . . .prayed for Spirit to come down, and it did, and bowled me over. Nothing can equal it in my experience."* (Retired Baptist woman.)

> *"At the end of the 'Saints Alive!' course, we were baptized in the Holy Spirit. I spoke about God for the first time in front of others; it felt like a door had just been knocked down. I felt all tingly and very happy, but weepy, and a feeling of wanting to be on my own."* (Anglican man of 29, a part–time cleaner.)

Some experienced what is called by many charismatics "resting in the Spirit", and by some Pentecostals "being slain in the Spirit". It occurs when an individual who is being prayed for falls to the ground and lies semi–conscious. This may last for only a few seconds but can be much longer.

> *"Our guest speaker held his hand six inches away from me and the power of the Holy Spirit came through him and I was slain in the Spirit (yippee!)."* (Baptist woman librarian of 29.)

> *"At a laying on of hands some people prayed for me with a priest, and I lay in the Spirit . . . I felt so full of love, like Jesus was holding my entire body in the palm of his hand. I had a warm glow and light was all around."*

Tongues (glossolalia) were mentioned by about a third of those who were filled with the Spirit:

"During lectures at the church on the Holy Spirit the leaders called down the Holy Spirit . . . he prayed over those who wished it to receive the gift and I began speaking in tongues." (Young Baptist woman.)

And this Roman Catholic woman received tongues a short while after her experience of the infilling of the Spirit:

"It was almost repeated when I was confirmed into the Catholic Church last year. I spoke in tongues — I felt a peace, almost an excess of peace! . . . There was nothing violent — no shaking or sudden rush — it was almost an overwhelming sense of peace and wellbeing. The presence of God . . . People noticed me 'glowing' the next day."

Healing

Many participants spoke of the possibility of healing through prayer, accompanied by the laying on of hands or anointing with oil, as an almost normal experience within the church. While this practice of the ministry of healing is common in charismatic churches it is by no means confined to them. 10% of those who had an unusual experience described a healing of themselves or someone they were close to. Instances come from all denominations:

"On a church holiday quite a few people were healed. A girl had eczema scars on her face, they were gone the next day. Someone was healed of diabetes. My friend had her ankle healed: physicians and doctors hadn't known what was wrong — she hadn't been able to run for three years." (Sixth form student in a community church.)

"I had been on crutches for a long time. I had problems with my knee. I went to the healing service and had my knee prayed for. That night as I went to bed, I felt my knee get warm. My friend felt my knee and said she could feel it. I felt my leg getting stronger and I put my crutches to one side. I felt something pulling me forward and I started walking — I felt no pain and I was not limping. To this day I have had no trouble with the knee." (38–year–old unemployed Anglican woman.)

"I was diagnosed with having a curvature of the spine. I was being medically observed and I had prayer for healing in the church service. The next time I had an X–ray I was discharged from

hospital because my spine was hardly bent at all." (Young Baptist
student.)

*"The pastor's wife had just come out of hospital and I thought that
. . . I would take a box of chocolates to cheer her up. I was in a great
deal of pain myself from a leg injury sustained six months earlier
which had not responded to treatment. During my visit the pastor's
wife asked if I was in pain — it must have shown on my face . . . I
agreed for the pastor and his wife to lay hands on my knee and
pray. Before I left their home my knee was much better and within
a couple of days was completely healed."* (Retired Baptist man.)

Intuition

The sense of being directed in a certain path or being given some
knowledge which will be of importance is common to Christians.

*"When I was 18 I was working in a residential hotel and we had a
Baptist minister's wife in her 70s staying. I was very fond of her.
One morning I woke up and had to go straight to the hotel — she
was on the floor in a state of collapse. I was driven — I just had to
be there. Had she been thinking of me very strongly — she was a
devout Christian and we had a strong bond? I didn't see it as
dramatic until . . . years later when I was nursing and was aware
that having that intuitive feel for patients and people was very
helpful. But it disappears if you're stressed and uptight."*

DREAMS

3% of people said that dreams were a main factor in their period of
turning to God, and 4% of men and 2% of women said they had been a
supporting factor, but they are of course not confined to this period of
their Christian pilgrimage.

14% of those who had an unusual experience described a dream or
vision:

*"In my home in Ghana I had a dream — that unless I marry the
man I lived with, I would not have a baby. I acted as commanded
in the dream, got pregnant, but had a miscarriage."*

*"I had a dream . . . that I was in church, only I was much older and
I looked like my mum. Then I noticed my friend John who was lay
reader dressed as a vicar. I felt the Lord saying to me that John was
to be a vicar, although not for some time yet. Later when I told him*

*my dream he was amazed for only the previous day he had felt God
telling him to give up his job and go into the ministry."*
(39–year–old assistant librarian.)

AVOIDING DANGER

The escape from danger is often associated with divine intervention —
either in the sense that God prevents a catastrophe or that God is to be
greatly thanked for a narrow escape. A few described such events like
this Roman Catholic woman teacher of 36:

*"Driving to Oxford a car came round the bend on my side of the
road. It lifted over the top of my car. I don't know how I missed it
but neither me or the car were damaged. Made me more aware of
the saints and death."*

EXTRAORDINARY HAPPENINGS

All the things which are described in this chapter have been far out of
the ordinary to the people describing them. This section tells the stories which do not fit into any other category!

*"The clock on the mantelpiece hasn't worked for fifteen years. My
husband when discussing with me the spiritual things said, 'If that
clock works then I'll believe that God is'. Approximately two
weeks later I ordered the clock to go using the authority of Jesus.
The clock operated then for about three to four weeks. That
encouraged my faith."* (42–year–old shop owner from a New
Church.)

*"I was sitting in the bath pondering over: 'Why is there suffering!'
when a voice said 'up to you'. It left me shivering and cold and
definitely confirmed my Christian faith beyond all doubt although
I have a questioning mind."* (33–year–old man from an ecumenical
church.)

*"I was feeling angry at myself and the world. One night I felt my
mind rising quickly towards a bright orange light and felt myself
going 'home' and then falling back, after which I felt more relaxed.
It was many years later that I heard of 'out of the body
experiences'."* (Anglican housewife of 40.)

A large number spoke of a consciousness of the presence of Christ,

though few had such a vivid experience as this Catholic woman on a
station platform:

> *"I felt very low (early morning Clapham Common — commuting). I
> was walking along and heard my name spoken aloud and at the
> same time I felt a hand gently come to rest on my right shoulder. I
> looked round expecting to see someone, but there was only empty
> space. Inside I knew it was Jesus — which was rather confusing
> because I didn't believe in Jesus except as a fictitious character in
> stories."*

THE OCCULT

Some of the people in the survey had been involved with spiritualism
and various forms of occultism in their past, though none apparently
had been deeply committed to it. Their experiences illustrate the dan-
gers of these practices and the experience of deliverance out of them.

> *"I had dabbled with the occult in my teens and as I felt the peace
> of the Holy Spirit flood through me . . . it freed me from a fear I had
> of the unknown darkness."* (Anglican housewife of 32.)

> *"We became involved in ouija boards and contacted a man who
> claimed to be born in 1832. The whole experience became highly
> dangerous . . . we spoke to Satan and were under his influence.
> When Jesus came into my life I was pleased to run into his arms."*
> (Baptist man of 29.)

> *"I came and told the vicar that I had asked Jesus into my life and
> he prayed with me. That night I woke up in a terrible battle (I had
> been involved with spiritualism). I was being torn apart when a
> voice — calm and full of authority — spoke, rebuking the spirits in
> the name of Jesus. They fled. I felt such peace I slept for the first full
> night in over 20 years."* (United Reformed Church woman teacher of
> 54.)

EXPERIENCES WITH THOSE WHO HAVE DIED

This phenomenon where someone is conscious of encountering someone who has died is well known:

> *"I was alone just a few weeks after my father–in–law had died and
> I was washing the kitchen floor when I saw him standing in the
> doorway looking very happy."* (Anglican housewife of 36.)

"About ten months after my husband's passing I went to bed and my husband lay by my side. He looked young and his chest was bare . . . When I awoke next morning I felt comforted. Was it a dream or . . . ?" (Retired evangelical housewife.)

It is extraordinarily difficult to evaluate these experiences. For most people they were entirely positive, especially those which were "charismatic". They described them as strengthening their faith, and 9% of those who had had an out of the ordinary religious experience said it had even initiated or rekindled it. Only 9% said they were unaffected by what had happened to them.

These experiences were nearly always highly significant to the people concerned and a very real part of their Christian journey. However strange or even distasteful some of them may seem they have to be taken seriously. Those recounting them often fear scepticism or mockery and the church must show the utmost understanding and acceptance.

It may well be that the anonymity of filling in a questionnaire enabled those in the survey to tell of these experiences in a way which they would hesitate to do to someone they knew. These happenings were a very real part of the spiritual journeys of 43% and deeply meaningful to those concerned. People often had difficulty picking the right words to describe what they found almost indescribable.

CHAPTER 11

The public profession of faith

What kind of "public profession of faith" did the participants make?

33% had been baptized — of these more than a quarter (28%) had been previously baptized as infants.

75% of the participants had been confirmed/received into membership/done an RCIA course (about a quarter of these had combined it with another declaration of faith — usually baptism).

Many, of course, had been baptized as infants (60%).

There was a marked difference between social groups. ABC1s were more likely to have been confirmed etc. compared with C2DEs (76% against 62%). Correspondingly 46% of C2DEs had been baptized compared with 29% of ABC1s.

Needless to say, there were a wide variety of reasons why people decided to make some sort of public statement of their commitment. Nearly a quarter said that they needed to show others that they were now Christians: "I wanted to stand up and be counted."

A similar number felt that this was the next logical step in their Christian pilgrimage:

"I wanted to be closer to God and more involved in the church."

Two people simply said "Why not!" — they had found God in Christ and now needed to take the obvious next step.

8% felt it was what one had to do to join the church. This was particularly marked among Roman Catholics where this was mentioned by 39%.

"It was a way of saying 'Thank you' for what I had received."

Several quoted scripture, "because it is stated in the Bible that if you believe you must be baptized". A few felt they needed to give something back to the church which had given so much to them.

Preparation

It was clear that any preparation before the profession would come at a particularly important time in the spiritual journeys of the participants and it was important to find out what the people we interviewed had thought of both the preparation and the profession itself.

Rather surprisingly 16% had had *no* instruction beforehand. The rest had on average about ten sessions — the longest was reported by two Catholics who had had fifty. The length of course varied greatly according to denomination — the average Methodist went to seven sessions while the average Catholic went to twenty–eight.

The great majority of Anglicans, Catholics, and Baptists had had some form of preparation, but the proportion was lower for the Methodists (78%) and the New Churches (53%).

17% had received one–to–one teaching and the rest had been in a group. A few who had been involved in groups mentioned that the course could have been tailored more to their personal needs. However this has to be balanced by the great benefit which people had found in being able to talk together. Possibly group meetings with an opportunity for one or two individual sessions would be best.

In the great majority of cases they were led by a minister, sometimes with lay help. This personal contact with the church leadership was seen as a benefit by many. They were coming rather hesitatingly into the life of the church and it made them feel valued. The friendship with the minister was greatly appreciated.

The great exception to this clerical leadership was the RCIA course which is discussed below in more detail.

Also, an Anglican matron from a residential home was in a small group led by lay people:

> "*I was taught by three committed Christians from church in my own home, which I found very relaxing and very informal. It was a very enjoyable experience.*

Commitment to the preparation had been remarkable — 95% had attended most or all the sessions.

There was also an extremely high level of satisfaction with these preparatory sessions. 95% rated them "helpful": it is likely that the ministers who led them would have been pleased with as high a rating for their sermons! When asked if there was anything which could have improved them, one suggestion was to make the course longer.

The courses seemed to achieve several purposes:
1. They enabled people to *discuss* the faith. This was seen by many as the most important part of the preparation, and the ability to talk about their newly emerging faith in a supportive environment was

invaluable. Most obviously found that to "talk about religion" was not something which was done in their ordinary life and the sense of relief was profound:

"We were all allowed our say and nobody laughed."

" . . .one could talk about one's faith . . . without feeling embarrassed and could explore what one believed."

It was particularly helpful if people talked about their uncertainties as well as their faith:

"You could talk to people who had the same doubts as yourself . . ."

"Even the vicar had trouble with some questions."

"It was very useful to hear problems the others had come across and to feel you weren't the only one who didn't understand everything!"

The importance of discussion was highlighted by the few negative comments, which showed how disappointed people were when this did not take place:

"The man knew a lot of theology but no real interaction happened . . . I was annoyed because we couldn't thrash things out."

"The vicar showed a filmstrip and followed a book course where personal guidance and videos would have been better."

2. They met the desire to *learn* about the Christian faith. "I felt more confident in what I was believing because of the knowledge and reading the Bible"; "having the Bible explained by a vicar was very, very helpful". Most seemed to want to grapple intellectually with what being a Christian means, but were not impressed by those "who spoke over our head in theological terms". This Methodist wanted more sparkle:

"Most of the sermons were about the church — history, dogma etc. They weren't personal or challenging or enthusiastic."

People seemed to want teaching about the heart of the Christian faith rather than what they regarded as peripheral:

"The subjects we discussed were boring such as, 'How the Bible was written', and 'How do different religions interact with each other?'."

> *"The course was more structured towards becoming a 'Methodist' — which I found interesting but irrelevant."*

3. The courses allowed people to *meet others* within the church. "I met a lot of nice people and made a lot of friends and it helped me to realize how friendly and close knit the Catholic community is". A deeper lesson had been learnt by this Catholic housewife of 44:

> *"As we shared in a personal way I began to see others' journey — it widened my understanding of who God is — how he loves and touches lives. I appreciated and came to know others as very special individual people."*

4. They helped people to begin to *experience the corporate nature of believing* — "there was a feeling of being drawn into the church". The sense that the group was on a journey of faith together was mentioned by some:

> *"we looked at religion from an adult point of view . . . we all had the same questions."*

5. Participants were helped to *enter into the culture of the church.* "They helped at a practical level with church etiquette"; "it taught me what things in church mean: i.e. symbols".

The forms of instruction were generally liked (95% of participants commented on this). Courses which had follow-up meetings *after* the public profession scored very highly on the "helpful" scale — nearly a half of participants kept going — often in a form of a Bible study group or house group. One person who had not had the chance of this said as much: "It would have been nice if the same group of people could have formed their own 'House Group'."

Perhaps preparation should always include some provision for follow-up sessions after the baptism/confirmation etc. (as is standard practice in the RCIA course).

The priorities in the preparation of candidates for baptism, confirmation etc. appear to be:

1 How to live as a Christian

— forming a relationship with God through Christ, and maintaining it through prayer, Bible reading, sacrament, and Christian action in the world.

2 How to live within the church

— helping people to become familiar with the church and its culture and providing opportunities for friendships to grow.

3 How to think as a Christian

— giving people sufficient theological knowledge to be able to explain their faith and think as Christians.

Other subjects are subsidiary: e.g. denominational teaching, history, and doctrine which is not earthed in the personal questions which participants are asking.

What did participants think of their profession of faith?

Participants were asked what they thought of their baptism/confirmation/reception etc.

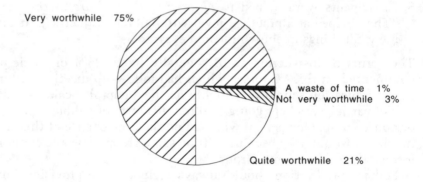

Fig. 20 Opinion of public profession of faith.

Baptism was seen as very worthwhile by 86% of those who had been baptized. One man was enthusiastic "even though it was in icy water". A young Anglican woman said:

"I was baptized unusually — in a river . . . I suppose not unnormally because Jesus was baptized in a river . . ."

"God's presence was apparent — not only to me . . . The prophecy spoken over me was very important and we very recently have seen some of that being confirmed." (Evangelical male teacher of 45.)

"The day I was baptized it was as if all from my inside had gone. I began crying as it was a feeling I couldn't describe or forget. It was as if I was washed and made fire inside." (Baptist nurse of 55.)

"When I was baptized at Easter I felt accepted by the whole community by way of their congratulations and wishes which made me feel part of the 'family'." (Catholic building labourer of 27.)

A woman of 35 looked to baptism to help her at a different level:

"From my occult days I felt unclean and that there was something still in me, and felt that being re–baptized would cleanse me."

The desire for some public sign of adult commitment and especially for baptism is very real, and adults coming or returning to faith who were baptized in infancy can find it difficult not to be able to celebrate their baptism. There is a need for those churches which practise infant baptism to help such people to "reclaim" their baptism.

Nowadays adults often come from far outside the life of the church. The former pattern whereby nearly everybody could look back on a childhood spent within a church environment is disappearing. It is becoming less common for people to have some experience of the church as a child, to drift away in their teens and then return as a young adult. Some of the people in the survey had been baptized as infants and then had no further contact with the church for twenty, thirty or more years and this is likely to become more normal. When these people encountered God they often felt that baptism was the only rite which fully expressed what they had experienced. One woman of 54 put the dilemma clearly:

"I was christened as a baby . . . When I returned to God I decided to be baptized. I was asked to leave the church because it would cause embarrassment. The vicar, rather than facing the issue, asked for my resignation or a decision not to be baptized. I chose to leave."

Those who find faith in these circumstances need something liturgically dramatic and psychologically satisfying to match the major changes which they feel God has made in their lives. They have the courage to want to confess this publicly and to follow what they see as a scriptural imperative. They need something which helps their spiritual life forward rather than being made to feel as though they are being disloyal. A failure to address this question adequately explains in part the movement which the survey shows towards the churches which baptize those previously baptized as infants.

The renewal of baptismal vows is now common in some churches, and some of the RCIA rites seek to fulfil this desire, but the pastoral needs of the people concerned must be given full weight.

Confirmation came a close second with 74% rating it very worthwhile:

"A magical experience — the church itself, the incense, robes, singing, sunlight through stained glass — I felt as though God was pleased." (Anglican woman poet of 40.)

"I experienced the Holy Spirit in it — commissioning me in a new way. I felt as though I was being given something new for God. He was giving me power and strength to go and do it . . . scriptural too — anointing and laying on of hands." (Roman Catholic woman piano teacher of 50.)

An unemployed Anglican woman had been able to tell her faith story at her confirmation. It had an effect:

"People came up to me and wanted to know if Jesus could love them. They wanted to know more about him. I made a lot of Christians through my talk and I was declaring God's love."

A Roman Catholic man of 40 had a similar experience:

"One person who was present at my confirmation/holy communion also was 'converted' the following year — and said it was my example that inspired him."

9% had found that their baptism or confirmation had been an opportunity to speak about their faith to non–Christians.

Reception into church membership as a sign of adult faith did not get as much praise as being baptized or confirmed:

"Our reception into church membership was a waste of time. It was irrelevant since it was done in a council meeting — behind closed doors so to speak."

"It hasn't made any difference to me personally."

However, many Catholics did find "reception" meaningful:

"I found actually becoming a Catholic a great comfort and felt I was joining a body of people who were strong and loyal to their faith."

At a time of adult public commitment there seems to be a need to have a ceremony which is both dramatic and colourful. Reception into membership can have a somewhat bureaucratic feel which may detract from this, and churches where this is the normal practice may need to see if there is any substitute or additional rite which can provide what is needed. There was also a rather higher level of unhappiness with the preparation compared with that given for baptism or confirmation. Some ministers seem to have given an introduction to the church and the denomination when people looked for more direct help with their Christian life.

THE RITE OF CHRISTIAN INITIATION OF ADULTS

The preparation course which we looked at specifically was the RCIA. It was different from most of the others in a number of ways:

1. It was largely specific to one denomination. The RCIA is the course which is recommended throughout the Roman Catholic Church (only a handful of Anglicans also claimed to have been part of a catechumenate).

2. It was much longer than the others — averaging over twenty-eight sessions taken over almost a year.
   It was clear that for many the RCIA group had become such a fixed point in their lives that they missed it when it came to an end:

   "After the course I felt that I needed more but after you have been 'received' there is nothing more for you." (36–year–old male design manager.)

   "Meetings had become an important part of my life. If they stopped suddenly then joining the church would be to lose close involvement with other parishioners." (Female teacher of 41.)

   This may be a point which needs to be addressed by those running catechumenate courses.

3. It is intended to be led by lay people though it was clear that clergy were involved in the majority of cases. 42% reported that the groups they had attended were led by clergy, 21% said it had been a mixture of both clergy and lay people, and 37% said that they had been led only by lay men and women.
   Although there were many who appreciated being with a priest:

   "I enjoyed every moment I spent with Father." (61–year–old woman shop assistant.)

   the presence of lay people was also mentioned approvingly by many:

   "I am sure that without their dedication and time, a great many

*of us receiving instruction would not be in God's House today
and I thank them from the bottom of my heart for helping me."*
(49–year–old roofer.)

*"Other Catholics shared their faith with me and listened to my
questions and fears without pressure."* (Female typist of 45.)

4. The course is very open–ended with much emphasis on helping the
people in the group to discover the answers as they make their pilgrimage. Some people liked this:

*"I could share my feelings and return to the support of the
group."* (40–year–old male government officer.)

*"The RCIA classes were most informal, informative, and
friendly. The subjects covered the whole gamut of the Christian
faith."* (Retired Catholic man.)

However, others wanted more "instruction" (which is surprising in
view of the length of the course):

*"If it had been structured differently then perhaps it might have
been worthwhile."*

*"It could definitely be improved by teaching more about the
Catholic religion — this was felt strongly by all converts and was
even expressed at the diocesan meeting from all groups taking
part."* (57–year–old housewife.)

*"Although I enjoyed attending the classes I felt to some extent
questions were not being answered."* (43–year–old female factory
worker.)

*"More instructional classes as I feel/felt a void — wanting to
know more but unable to do anything about it."* (Male manager
of 36.)

*"They did not teach me anything new about the Bible, of a new
interpretation. Also did not teach about Catholicism."* (Male
accounts officer of 42.)

5. It was interspersed with public services (the "rites") which marked
the completion of one phase of the course and of the person's journey into faith and the beginning of another.
The course is so structured that the group continues to meet after
the profession of faith (which is nearly always at Easter) and 88%
found that this was a helpful element in the course: "It reinforced

that the public declaration was not the end but only the beginning". 18% said that the group had continued to meet beyond the official end of the course.

6. RCIA groups tended to be larger than most (averaging ten instead of the seven of the others). This could lead to some sense of not having their agenda addressed: "time for one–to–one instruction would have been very helpful". As one said, "the groups could have been smaller".

However it has to be said that the overwhelming experience of this very thorough preparation course was positive. No less than 98% said it was "helpful".

Disappointments

Needless to say not everyone was euphoric about the process of initiation. A few were disappointed:

"I expected to feel different but I didn't." (Anglican nurse of 28.)

"I knew in my heart it was something I must do, but did not attach to it the feeling of 'wonderful' that lots of people called it. Baptism was only a follow–up to giving my life which was the really wonderful thing." (Baptist man of 38.)

But they were very much the exception. A woman of 39 expressed what most felt:

"It was the best thing I had ever done in my life — it felt so right."

A *personal epilogue*

For more than ten years I have had a dream. It is of the churches of Britain being so renewed in their thinking and their praying that they bring good news to the nation sensibly and sensitively.

In 1980 the Nationwide Initiative in Evangelism called for "intelligent and effective evangelism". As I evangelized and looked at others doing the same I was conscious that we knew far too little about the end product of evangelism to do it intelligently and as a result much of it was ineffective.

Evangelization needs to be founded upon fact rather than fantasy. Many industrial companies spend 15–20% of their turnover on research and development. The churches in this country have a turnover of many millions and yet I doubt if the amount spent on research is as much as half of one per cent. As a result money is wasted, the time of Christians is squandered, and most important of all, people do not hear the good news of God in Christ in a way they can respond to.

The need for a spiritual basis for our nation is too urgent to be left to the latest bright idea or the preferences and drive of a few individuals. It was for this reason that I tried to get this research off the ground. God has given us many new adult Christians and we do not always see what they can teach us. It is to them that this report is dedicated for the greater glory of God.

As we close this part of the research I have certain "long term" prayers:

- *that the evaluation of what it is doing will become normal for the Christian church and so we allow the Holy Spirit to lead us into truth. In particular I pray that the avenues of research which this survey has opened up may be explored by others and their conclusions help to guide the Church.*

- *that we continue to honour and learn from those who are beginning the journey of faith — "and a little child shall lead them".*

- *that Christians become so light-footed that we are prepared to change readily in response to the guiding of the Holy Spirit.*

But my short term prayer is for this report and all that may flow from

110

it, that it may be of value to both local and national churches in helping them to evangelize in a way which is more aware of the person
who is being evangelized. It is this genuine care we have for those outside the life of the Church which prevents evangelization becoming
proselytization.

At Christmas 1991 I sat down for a week and read straight through
all the 10,000 or more pages from the questionnaires that had been
returned. It was thrilling to read of lives put together by the power of
God, of ordinary people with extraordinary stories, and above all of a
new realization of the grace of God which is poured out on us in such
variety. In *Alice's Adventures in Wonderland* by Lewis Carroll, the
lobster sings,

> *"Will you, wo'n't you, will you, wo'n't you, will you join the dance?*
> *"Will you, wo'n't you, will you, wo'n't you, wo'n't you join the*
> *dance?"*

The tunes of the Spirit play, and we invite others to join in — but first
we need to make sure that we ourselves are responsive to the heavenly
music.

For myself this research has had many uncertainties and a curious
mixture of anxiety and hope. I humbly offer it to the Church with the
prayer that it may help to extend the Kingdom of our Lord and our
God.

Appendix

This research grew out of work done by John Finney in the early 1980s in which about 450 people were asked questions about their Christian pilgrimage. The results were both unexpected and interesting but the methodology was so haphazard that it would have been unwise to build upon the results (they are recorded on page 126 of *Understanding Leadership*, DLT 1989). In 1988 he wished to discover any other work in this area, but found very little apart from the testimonies of individuals. The Evangelism Committee of the British Council of Churches were approached and they were cautiously enthusiastic. With their blessing funds were sought which would enable the survey to be carried out.

The main area of research was:

"a) to examine the spiritual journeys by which people are finding faith in God through Christ at the present

  b) to draw conclusions from this research on the comparative merits of different evangelistic methods."

A subsidiary area of research was:

"c) to collate work which has already been done on the motivations of those attending church"

Funds were obtained from:

The Central Board of Finance of the Church of England (Church House Fund)	£20,000
The British and Foreign Bible Society	£20,000
Nottingham City Mission	£2,000
British Council of Churches	£1,000
Board of Mission and Unity of the General Synod	£500
Cyril Black Trust	£100
Diocese of Salisbury	£50

The Project is enormously grateful for all those who contributed and enabled this venture to begin.

From the beginning great help had been given by Bible Society and it was agreed that it would employ a researcher to do the field work on behalf of the British Council of Churches Evangelism Committee — and latterly Churches Together in England which part way through the survey became the ecumenical instrument appropriate to England. The inclusion of the Roman Catholic Church in that body gave the survey an added dimension.

A Monitoring Group under the chairmanship of Canon Michael Rees was set up by the British Council of Churches and subsequently adopted by Churches Together in England. The members were:

Canon Michael Rees: former Chief Secretary of the Church Army and Moderator of the B.C.C. Evangelism Committee, and now Diocesan Missioner in the Diocese of Chester.

Dr John Boyes: Executive Director of the Christian Brethren Research Fellowship (John died in February 1992 and we missed his incisive mind).

Mr George Georgiou: Senior Research Officer of Bible Society

Miss Pat Jones: Assistant General Secretary to the Catholic Bishops' Conference.

The Revd Geoffrey Pearson: former secretary of the B.C.C. Evangelism Committee. Vicar of Roby, Liverpool.

Mr Ken Rose: former secretary of the B.C.C. Evangelism Committee. Member of Team Spirit. (Secretary of the Monitoring Group.)

Ms Pam Hanley was appointed as full–time researcher for fifteen months from 1 October 1989. After a period of familiarization in which she met many engaged in mission as leaders and evangelists, a questionnaire was produced. Students from the following theological colleges were trained in interviewing techniques and carried out 130 interviews:

> Chichester (Anglican)
> Cliff (Methodist)
> Crowther Hall (Anglican)
> Oscott (Roman Catholic)
> St Andrew's College (Presbyterian)
> St John's, Nottingham (Anglican)
> Spurgeon's (Baptist)
> Wesley House (Methodist)
> Westminster (United Reformed Church)

The remainder were carried out by Pam Hanley and John Finney to give a total of 151 face–to–face interviews.

A further 735 questionnaires were sent out by post and 313 of these were returned — a percentage of 43% which is very high for a survey of this nature involving a 22 page questionnaire.

A subsequent survey was made of 47 people who been through an RCIA course.

This total of 511 questionnaires form the basis of the survey.

The questionnaires were both quantitative and qualitative: i.e. participants were asked for narratives as well as facts. They had both to tick suggested answers and also to put down their thoughts and stories in their own words. It was therefore a considerable task for them — probably taking one to two hours. The thoroughness with which most answered the questionnaire was remarkable. In particular the qualitative questions which required them to tell their own story produced an abundance of riches.

It had been anticipated that the face–to–face interviews would produce deeper insights than the self–completion questionnaires. While this was probably correct in some cases it was certainly not generally true — the fact that the interviewer was not present meant that participants thought more carefully about their answers — possibly also they found it easier to write down their more personal thoughts than when they were face–to–face with an interviewer. There is also some evidence that participants were slightly more accurate in filling in a questionnaire regarding their present level of churchgoing etc. (a factor well known in all interviewing).

The names and addresses of those to be approached were obtained from the ministers of churches chosen at random from the national lists produced by the different denominations and the New Churches. The fact that Roman Catholic churches tend to have congregations more than three times larger than non–Catholic churches meant that fewer of them were approached than their national figures for churchgoing would suggest was appropriate. This, alongside the RCIA requirement, meant that the number of Catholics initially approached was less than might otherwise have been the case and a further 80 were approached later, with a response rate of about 60%. Conversely this factor tended to inflate the number of Methodist and Anglican churches approached because they have large numbers of rural churches. On the other hand those churches which baptize as adults those baptized as infants, primarily the Baptists and New Churches, tended to produce more names of those who had "made a public profession of faith" than others.

Despite these drawbacks, which tend to cancel each other out, and which are inevitable in any survey such as this, the figures in the survey represent all denominations in all parts of England, and are well within the bounds of statistical respectability.

The percentages in the report are based on all those who answered the question (i.e. those who did not answer a particular question are excluded from the calculations, for that question).

The field work for the survey was done in the period from March to June 1991, and the results computerized by Manchester Polytechnic. Pam Hanley then wrote her technical report and in the light of it John Finney wrote a draft of this report. The draft was then circulated to members of the Monitoring Group and others for their comments and additions.

It was appreciated from the beginning that merely producing a report was not going to be sufficient and an educational programme has been devised to enable Christians to understand what had been discovered, to change their attitudes as a result and produce an appropriate strategy for evangelizing their locality. A group was asked to produce educational material. This is centred upon material which is suitable for church leaders to use in their areas of responsibility — whether it be the training of ordinands and evangelists, encouraging intelligent evangelism in the local church or ordinary church members seeking to like out their lives more effectively as Christians.

Besides this report there are two further papers which are available from Churches Together in England or Bible Society.

1. The educational material which helps people to learn the main facts of the report and produce a pattern of mission for their churches:
   Available early 1993.
2. The Technical Report on the research. This was written by Pam Hanley at the end of her research and gives in greater detail the statistical findings of the research:
   Available immediately.